BUY TO LET

The Essential Guide

Melissa Perez

But To Let: The Essential Guide is also available in accessible formats for people with any degree of visual impairment. The large print edition and E-Book (with accessibility features enabled) are available from Need2Know. Please let us know if there are any special features you require and we will do our best to accommodate your needs.

First published in Great Britain in 2012 by
Need2Know
Remus House
Coltsfoot Drive
Peterborough
PE2 9BF
Telephone 01733 898103
Fax 01733 313524
www.need2knowbooks.co.uk

Contents

Introduction

Letting property out to a tenant is a practice that goes back thousands of years. At any given time, the number of people who cannot afford to buy their own home is greater than the ones who can. There is an ever-present demand for good properties to rent. The volatile nature of the property market does make investors apprehensive about tying up their money in properties. However, this doesn't dilute the fact that buying to let is a viable option to have a regular stream of income in the future. Even with the economy in doldrums, the buy to let investors are having a great time reaping off the fruit of their shrewd investment.

An investor looks at a piece of property from one of two views:

1. Capital growth.

2. Income stream.

If your objective is creating a stream of income that flows for the foreseeable future, then buy to let is the perfect option. From leading property tycoons and investors to the common man, an opportunity for investing and earning from buy to let properties is available to anyone.

You don't need to have a substantial capital to invest in buy to let. Through buy to let financing, the average person in the UK can buy a property and then earn the rent paid by the tenants. At the same time, benefits can be derived from capital growth.

In a perfect world, a person could walk into a finance company and obtain a loan for purchasing a buy to let property. Unfortunately, there are obstacles and pitfalls along the way that have to be overcome and avoided. An experienced investor with millions in the bank can overcome them easily, but those of you who are starting out need a helping hand.

This essential guide for buying to let is intended to provide the assistance the common man or woman would need to start investing. The first chapter explains the basics of buying to let investment and the principles that you need to learn. You need to learn the ropes of the trade before moving on to the advanced techniques and information.

As an essential guide, it is pertinent that its content covers all the aspects and areas of buying to let investment. The following chapters explain in detail the tax implications, benefits, potential pitfalls and tips for investing. Property investing is not a bed of roses and has to be tread on with caution. Before you take your first step, you have to be prepared.

Investing in property can be the easiest way to earn money, or to lose it. Read this informative and practical guide before you take the leap!

Chapter One

Buying to Let: Understanding the Concept

Although buying to let is not a brand new trend in the property market, it is gaining popularity as we speak. At the time of writing, it has been predicted that the buy to let market will grow significantly in the UK. Buying to let has many significant benefits, and if you are thinking of making a long-term investment in property, you should definitely go for buy to let.

Property rental is not a new activity. People have been letting out property to earn profits for several decades now. However, the availability of mortgages for this very purpose was unheard of. Moreover, tenants did not have any written short-term tenure, which made it hard for the landlords to evict them.

However, as time went by, some laws were passed which benefited both the tenants and the landlords, who found it easy to evict tenants on a short-term basis and arrange finance. This type of finance is now known as the buy to let mortgage. More on this to follow.

'Putting it simply, buy to let means that you buy a house that you will put up for rent.'

What is the meaning of buy to let?

Buy to let is a British term where 'let' refers to rent. Putting it simply, buy to let means that you buy a house that you will put up for rent. The finance comes from a buy to let mortgage. A buy to let mortgage is just like the simple house mortgage, except you use this one to purchase a property that you will let out on rent. In other words, you borrow money, buy a property, and then rent out the house to tenants in order to earn profits.

Although buy to let in its essence was being practised for many years, the exact term was created as a marketing tool for the Association of Residential Letting Agents (ARLA) back in 1995. A buy to let mortgage is different from a regular one in two ways.

Firstly, the amount of the down payment differs between the common mortgage and the buy to let mortgage. If you want to purchase a property for residential purposes, down payments can be as low as five percent. However, if you want to let your property, you have to put down at least 25% in down payment. That is a significant difference.

The second difference is that your income for mortgage eligibility is calculated in different manners depending on the type of finance you want to acquire. If you apply for a regular house mortgage, the bank will consider your income. On the other hand, in the case of a buy to let mortgage, the *expected* rent to be received in the future will also be included in your earnings, making it easier for you to get the mortgage. As house prices have increased at a considerable rate, buy to let mortgages have also increased significantly over the past five years.

History of the buy to let mortgage

It all started back in the 1970s. A law was passed in 1977, known as the Protection from Eviction Act, which was succeeded by the Rent Act in the same year. These legislations protected tenants from illegal eviction, as well as giving them the security of tenure. Although these laws protected the rights of the tenant, property rental became a loss-making business.

Both these acts were passed as the result of certain activities carried out by landlords, most notably Peter Rachman. They deliberately victimised and exploited their tenants so that they would leave. In their place, these landlords brought in new tenants with lower tenure security without charging any cap rent. Private owners took a back seat, but the state properties became highly ineffective in fulfilling the growing needs of houses as the population grew.

This dilemma was ultimately resolved by the passing of the 1988 Housing Act, which brought with itself the new concept of Assured Shorthold Tenancy. This resulted in property renting resurfacing again as a business that earned profits, as the tenants now had less security over their tenure, and landlords could now easily get rid of tenants who didn't want to leave!

Interestingly, this period also included the housing crash in the UK that went on for half a decade and resulted in many Brits being forced out of their own houses. The demand for rented properties increased, and the growth of buy to let proprietors became evident.

Moving on

Over time, buying to let has become one of the most successful industries in the UK. A survey conducted by the Association of Residential Letting Agents in 2005 revealed:

- 90% of the landlords committed to keep back their investment even if prices fell.

- 62% of landlords had long-term property investments (10 years or more).

- The average investment life was 16 years.

- 58% revealed the urge to make more investments in the future.

In 1997, the Council of Mortgage Lenders (CML) gathered statistics on buy to let in the UK, and they believed that these numbers were evidence of a boom in the economy. Another reason for the success of buy to let was that many landlords shifted towards commercial mortgages. This means they sought loans keeping their buy to let properties as collateral. Almost 40% of the buy to let proprietors were involved in commercial remortgaging.

Buy to let mortgages have increased significantly since the start of this millennium. The year 2007 saw the growth of wholesale lenders. Large banks like HBOS also became buy to let wholesale lenders. These lenders sold repackaged mortgage securities to other lenders at higher rates. However, these securities eventually caused buy to let lenders to fall in number in the UK. In fact, these lenders charged such low prices on their loans that buy to let mortgages became cheaper than housing mortgages!

'Over time, buying to let has become one of the most successful industries in the UK.'

Ultimately, the buy to let market saw its peak in 2008, reaching £27.2 billion lending money! However, it took only what seemed like moments to crash down to just £8.5 billion in 2009. Not only were lenders hesitant to give out loans, they also increased the value of the mortgages. These valuations dropped significantly, by almost 50%, in 2009. Since then, the UK government has passed laws not only to protect the rights of the customers, but also to make sure that mortgage values do not drop down to dangerous levels. In fact, many people blame the whole buy to let system for rising house prices. You may be surprised to know that most properties in the UK are being bought by buy to let investors, which many believe poses a threat both to the banking and the housing industry.

Many of these investors are not UK-based citizens, but come from places like Saudi Arabia, France and Italy to buy property in London, which is a significant contributor to inflation. Although small-scale proprietors have appeared on the scene, the market is still dominated by professional investors and landlords. Many people also claim that in 2012, the buy to let market will once again reach its peak, as it shows signs of potential growth.

'The buy to let market saw its peak in 2008, reaching £27.2 billion lending money!'

Why do people engage in buy to let?

Buy to let is a business that is based on investments, and any such economic activity has the benefit of monetary returns and profits. Many claim that since buy to let is an economic activity in the property industry, it is far more reliable (in terms of returns) than the stock market.

You can deposit money in the bank as well, but it will not provide you the same earnings as property rentals. As a buy to let property owner, not only will you have a constant income from rent that tenants pay you, you will also benefit if house prices rise. It is a great method of wealth accumulation, and perhaps the main reason why buy to let landlords have increased in number in the UK.

However, as in all forms of investment, buy to let also runs the risk of loss. It is based on speculation, where you *estimate*:

- The rent that you are likely to receive.

- The property can be sold in the future if prices rise.

- The earnings from the rent received will be greater than the cost of mortgage.

If for some reason the landlord fails to pay the mortgage, the bank has the right to seize his/her property and auction it to cover their costs.

Do not be alarmed! All types of businesses and profit ventures have some risks associated with them. They are risks and not *restrictions*. You can continue buying to let despite these complications by following some considerations. That's why this book was written — to help you make wise decisions and overcome all obstacles in buying to let.

Some factors to consider

People who apply and become eligible for borrowing finance for buy to let have some common options to choose from, such as:

- Fixed
- Variable
- Tracker

Please remember that the rates would be different (more, to be clear) from the normal housing mortgages. If you have deposited a substantial amount, you may be able to borrow finance on an interest-only basis.

The following factors are crucial to a successful buy to let investment. Please note that this is only a brief introduction, as all these features will be thoroughly explained in the coming chapters.

- Taxes – When you engage in buying to let, you will be taxed on your earnings. You will be charged with an income tax, but if your earnings exceed a significant proportion, you may probably have to pay a profit tax as well. The tax is usually gauged at 22% or 40%.
- Legal requirements – Requirements for buying to let are relatively straightforward. You need to pay a minimum 20% deposit, and you need to have a minimum income as well. The minimum income rate is not fixed. You would also need to assure the individual/company you are borrowing from

'As a buy to let property owner, not only will you have a constant income from rent that tenants pay you, you will also benefit if house prices rise.'

that the expected rental income is sufficient to pay the monthly mortgage instalments. Usually, the rent earnings have to be 125% of the borrowing amount.

- Insurance – If you are a property owner, you have to pay insurance on the house. Regular property insurance policies may not work, and you would have to get the required landlord's policy.

Summing Up

- The term 'buy to let' means purchasing a property that is then rented out to paying tenants.

- A buy to let mortgage is the same in principle as an ordinary house mortgage, although the percentage of down payment required for buy to let properties can differ significantly. As a prospective landlord you may be expected to put down up to 25% as a down payment against the 5% home owners are required to invest.

- In the 70s, two significant laws were passed to help protect the rights of tenants against unscrupulous landlords, such as the infamous Peter Rachman.

- Buy to let property owners not only benefit from a constant income from rent, but also from increases in house prices.

- Buy to let investment, as with any investment, is not without its risks – failure to make mortgage payments on a buy to let house means the bank can seize the property and auction it in order to cover their costs.

Chapter Two

How to Get Started and What's Involved

You have to understand the whole business if you want to be successful in buy to let. Although it is a great financial prospect, it will consume your time, money and energy immensely as you deal with all the research and the large volume of paperwork. However, if you are gifted with the talent of managing property, you could become a significant player in the market in a small amount of time.

Before considering the prospect of buying property for letting, you have to conduct a self-assessment. Do you have what it a takes to be a landlord? Ask yourself this question all the time. And let me remind you, this is not a one man show. Property letting is a complete network or a system that you cannot go through without some people on your side. There is a wide range of people out there that you have to deal with, including agents, lenders, brokers, legal officers, engineers, tax officials, and, most importantly, the tenants.

Not only do you need to select the right kind of people to work with, you should also have the mindset to deal with them effectively. Good leadership skills, along with a critical attitude, are required for successful property management. Once again, ask yourself, *do you have what it takes*? With that said, let us list down some important things you require before starting your buy to let business.

'Do you have what it a takes to be a landlord? Ask yourself this question all the time.'

Planning

You cannot proceed without proper planning if you want to step into the buy to let industry. It is a serious business that cannot be started without serious consideration. To aid you in effective planning, you can use the expertise of lawyers, accountants, tax officials and property specialists. Their advice will help you invaluably before you embark on your journey.

They will also help you look at each area in its proper perspective, and they will also ensure that you leave no corner unchecked. After consulting with the professionals, you can then analyse all the information presented to you, as well as think objectively whether this business suits you or not. Proper planning also helps you to get ahead of all unforeseen problems that may surface as you move along.

'Successful research also depends upon keeping a close eye on the market in which you are operating.'

Market research

The demand for rented homes is ever increasing, and based on the situation up to now, it is quite safe to say that the demand will continue forever. Chances are that whichever house you put up for rent will attract tenants automatically. However, since there are countless investors who are already established in the business, you will have to make sure that what you are offering helps you gain entry and take root in the market.

It is not inaccurate to say that the amount of rent you are likely to receive depends significantly on the level of research you are willing to undertake in terms of the location, the type of property, the type of tenants, and the rent itself. Successful research also depends upon keeping a close eye on the market in which you are operating. That will greatly help you in viewing the areas and the properties that are doing well among the tenants.

Consulting local estate agents also helps, as they can provide you information on the resident-favourite spots, along with the rent levels in different locations. There are also property search agents, who are specialists at finding the best properties that tenants will love. You can also search the Internet to find all this information easily.

Things you need to consider while conducting market research include:

Location

If anything can determine the success of your buy to let venture, it is the location of the property. To understand this point further, think about where you live. Are you comfortable in your house? Yes or no, and why so? You will definitely love a house that has shopping facilities, transport services, hospitals and schools nearby. Plus, it should be connected to the major locations in the city.

Usually, people are willing to pay good amounts to live in such locations, and if you manage to buy a property in these areas, you are likely to succeed in your project. If you get your location right, then enjoy. Otherwise, be prepared to make mortgage payments on empty properties!

The tenants

Another crucial factor in your research is your target market, i.e. what kind of tenants you are looking for. Singles would have different housing requirements as compared to families. Moreover, retired citizens will probably not look for the same factors when choosing a house as young professionals do.

Consulting estate agents will help you determine what kind of property different people require and whether these demands are being met or not. It is highly possibly that you can find a gap in the market, and filling that gap will give you endless benefits.

The property

There are several kinds of commercial properties and they all suit different types of tenants. For example, singles will usually look for a studio apartment, whereas a family will usually require a house with at least two bedrooms and close proximity to schools, hospitals and shops. The property you choose must have everything that your target audience is looking for.

Apart from the kind of property you will purchase, it is also important to determine whether it will be newly built or old. Old houses look beautiful and appeal to many people. However, they do have a greater need of maintenance

'If you get your location right, then enjoy. Otherwise, be prepared to make mortgage payments on empty properties!'

than a newly built house. Only go through this extra hassle if you know that there is a demand in the market for such homes. Otherwise you will waste both your time and energy.

Purchasing the property

After determining the type of house you will buy to let, you will have to decide how to buy it. Firstly, you will have to arrange the necessary finance. The market price of the property is not the only expense that you will have to bear, but also the costs of development, maintenance and tax. The most common way to buy a house for commercial purposes is using a buy to let mortgage.

'The market price of the property is not the only expense that you will have to bear, but also the costs of development, maintenance and tax.'

As mentioned in the previous chapter, you have many types of buy to let mortgages depending on your need. However, do remember that a buy to let mortgage is usually more expensive than a residential mortgage, and the lenders will also ask for a higher deposit.

You have to usually pay 25% deposit, though the amount can vary anywhere between 15-30%. It is difficult to find buy to let finance in the market, and that is why you have to pay a large deposit. However, if you are willing to pay a minimum of 5% above the required deposit, you will have a lot of options available as far as the lenders are concerned. Plus, you will probably get a lower mortgage rate for every extra 5%.

Apart from the purchase price, there are several other costs that you have to bear, such as:

- Management costs.
- Insurance.
- Furnishing.
- Mortgage repayments if you're unable to find tenants.
- Profit tax if you sell the house.
- Income tax.
- Stamp duty.
- Legal fees.

You need to prepare a well-calculated budget to avoid losing any unnecessary money.

Your responsibilities

After purchasing the property, you have to manage it properly as well. You will again have to think whether you have what it takes or not. A significant part of the task is taking care of the legal requirements of a landlord. By this we mean the health and safety issues, as well the fair treatment of tenants.

Your responsibilities as a landlord will include:

Providing adequate furnishings

Furniture and furnishings in your property should be fireproof, as required by the Furniture and Furnishings Amendment Regulations 1993. The following items, especially those made before 1988, should immediately be replaced:

* Bedroom furniture like beds and futons.
* Children's furniture.
* Garden tables and chairs.
* Cushions and pillows.

Old furniture that was made before 1950 does not fall under this law, along with carpets, sleeping bags, blankets, pillow cases and curtains. Most of these products do have stamps and labels that show which regulations the manufacturers follow. Just make sure that the furniture is fire resistant to avoid any mishaps, which can force you to pay heavy fines or even face imprisonment.

'A significant part of the task is taking care of the legal requirements of a landlord. By this we mean the health and safety issues, as well the fair treatment of tenants.'

Utilities

Although provisions for gas, water and electricity will be made by the government, a good landlord has to ensure that the tenants face no inconvenience or danger while benefiting from these utilities. You must provide a gas safety certificate to your tenants, and conduct regular maintenance and servicing of the gas equipment at least once a year.

Failure to do this can result is explosion and poisoning, and you will get into serious trouble. That is why all the gas equipment must be maintained properly, and you must always inform the occupants about their correct usage. In line with this point, you also have to ensure that the electric wiring in the building is in proper condition.

Old wiring must be checked and repaired frequently, and you should also have an inspection each year. Document all the electric tests and keep them with you for future reference so that you can prove that you were responsible enough as a landlord.

Legal agreements

You will also have to draw up written agreements with your tenants based on the Assured Shorthold Tenancy. The agreements will include things like:

- The names of both parties.
- The address of the house.
- The start and end date of the agreement.
- The amount of rent that has to be paid.
- When the rent has to be paid.
- When can it be increased legally.
- All the charges that have to borne by both parties.
- Responsibilities of both parties.

The tenure of the residents will be decided by both parties, but if the term is three years or more, a deed has to be drawn. Moreover, if you want to terminate the contract, you have to inform the tenants two months in advance.

You also need to know that it is illegal to discriminate against tenants. You cannot charge high rent or terminate them unfairly. Also, you cannot force them to pay a higher initial deposit, nor deprive them of their legal rights. Most importantly, you cannot refuse a person with a disability to live in the house, nor can you evict him/her illegally. You cannot even stop the tenant from making changes in the property to suit a disabled lifestyle.

You also have to draw up a landlord inventory. This is another important document that lists all the materials in the house kept by the landlord to be used by the tenants without any restriction. It also lists down their condition when the residents enter the house and after they leave.

Both the parties should discuss the inventory carefully and agree on the details to avoid any complications. You can review the inventory every three months by giving a notice at least one day before you plan to visit. However, it is preferable that you conduct this examination on the day when the tenants move out.

Finally, you always have the option of managing the property yourself, or hiring someone to take care of it. Employing someone to take on this responsibility will prove to be beneficial if you live in another city or country, or you have a busy work schedule (where buying to let is a side business for extra income). In such circumstances, you can always find an agent to manage the house while you are away.

On the other hand, if you have more than one letting property, then managing them will become your job. Consult different letting agents and see what kind of services they provide before hiring one. A good letting agent will handle responsibilities like:

- Inspecting and drawing up the landlord inventory.
- Dealing with the tenants on day-to-day issues.
- Collecting the deposit and rent.

'Both the parties should discuss the inventory carefully and agree on the details to avoid any complications.'

Finding the tenants

Once you have selected a property, you need someone to rent it. Finding the right kind of tenants and making them agree to a favourable rent is not an easy task, so be prepared! Many landlords who are new to the trade hire the services of a letting agent. The reason for this is that a first-time landlord will not have the firmness and confidence to deal and negotiate with the tenants as effectively as an experienced letting agent can.

Some of the functions that a good letting agent can perform for you are:

- Searching and analysing the potential tenants.
- Preparing your agreements.
- Managing the property.
- Inspecting the property regularly and conducting repairs.
- Collecting the rent and transfering the funds to you.
- Offering expert advice on matters of tenancy.
- Enquiring about the tenants (references from previous landlords, bank statements etc.).

If, on the other hand, you want to base all on your income on the rent received and become a full-time landlord, you might as well conduct all these activities yourself. Finding the tenants also requires some advertising.

'Finding the right kind of tenants and making them agree to a favourable rent is not an easy task, so be prepared!'

Documents and deposit

Once you have found the right customers, you will ask them to pay a deposit. This is usually equivalent to two months' rent, and the idea behind the payment is to protect you from any substantial damage by the tenant, or if he/she does not pay you the rent. However, this is not a simple give and take issue. Documentation is necessary in the payment and receipt of the deposit. The reason for the payment and the date for its repayment are to be agreed upon by all the parties involved.

You have to return the amount of the deposit agreed by you and the tenant prior to the payment if he/she pays the rent on time and if no significant damage to the property occurs. If you decide to keep back part or the complete deposit, inform the occupants in the most suitable time. You should do so in writing, stating clearly the amount you are withholding and the reason for your actions.

Better still, make written calculations or provide receipts of the cost of the damage and repairs to make the whole process as smooth as possible. When you draw up agreements and maintain receipts, not only do you resolve any issues related to the deposit easily, but you also avoid legal action. Since 2007, a law has been passed that requires landlords to handle matters related to the tenant's deposit fairly, otherwise you will be in a lot of trouble.

It doesn't end there

Even after finding the tenants and receiving the deposit, there is a lot of work left to do! Who is your tenant? A paying guest and you always prepare the house when the guests arrive! Make sure that before the tenants move in, the house is thoroughly clean and presentable. You have to inform the tax department, the mail office and the utility centres about the change of address. You also have to prepare some spare keys for the tenants.

Once they move in, give them a tour of the house while instructing them how things work (such as locks and security alarms). Ask them to resolve any queries they have before they settle down. Finally, take the meter readings and show them to the residents. Hand over the keys and wish them luck.

'Make sure that before the tenants move in, the house is thoroughly clean and presentable.'

Summing Up

- Being successful in the buy to let industry will involve you committing an immense amount of time and energy, as well as money, as you deal with the necessary research and paperwork.

- Being a landlord requires a lot of planning. It's essential to conduct proper market research before purchasing a property.

- Once you've purchased a property you have to be able to manage it effectively and undertake all your responsibilities as landlord with regards to your tenants' safety and legal rights.

- Documents and policies between landlord and tenant must be drawn up and agreed to by both parties, so misunderstanding and disagreements when the rental contract comes to an end are avoided.

- Employing the services of a reputable letting agent to help you deliver the services required and perform your responsibilities as a landlord can be invaluable.

Chapter Three

Reasons to Invest in Buying to Let

Overview

We now move to the section where we will be discussing some positive reasons for investing in a buy to let property/properties. You have now grasped the basic concept of buying to let and you also know the responsibilities and tasks expected of the landlord. But you should also remember that it is *not* a scheme to get rich overnight. You should always see buying to let as a long-term investment. This means that in the short run, there will be times where you have to spend money from your own pocket instead of earning anything, and you will also have to go through a lot of hassle to get things done.

This is especially true for dealing with the tenants and the letting agencies. All investments run some risks, and buying to let is no exception. It could be that you may not be able to find (or replace) tenants, leaving your property empty. No rent would be earned, but you would still have to pay the mortgage, taxes and maintenance costs. An empty buy to let property can really strike a blow to your finances, leaving you in an adverse liquidity position.

Moreover, it has been observed in the past couple of years, that it is not necessary and definite for property rates to rise over time. It was estimated that between March 2002 and November 2007, the rate at which housing prices rose, fell by almost 15%. It also speculated that if house prices continue to fall in 2012 at, let's say 5%, then a third of all buy to let landlords will owe more on their mortgage than the actual value of the house!

'Remember that it is *not* a scheme to get rich overnight. You should always see buying to let as a long-term investment.'

The rent yield is also an important factor that must be analysed by the new property owners, or those who are planning to enter the market. Last year, the average yield in the UK was 5.1%, but this still does not give you an accurate picture. Yields vary from place to place, and you will notice that even when rents are high, yields can be low. This is due to two reasons. Firstly, tenants were not able to, or simply did not pay their rents on time, and a large portion went in arrears.

Secondly, the cost of residence can be high, and this causes the rent yields to fall. But rents are expected to rise in the future as well, as young people especially will face a shortage of homes. Apart from the rising house prices, it is also difficult for young people to get a house mortgage. Not everyone understands economics and the market conditions, and you will always hear mixed reactions when it comes to buying to let. Therefore, the logical question that flows out of the discussion is as follows . . .

Is this the right time to invest?

Many economic commentators are showing their hesitation about the prospects of the buy to let business. If you consider house prices, inflation and mortgage values, then these inhibitions are not entirely baseless. However, there is a continual rise in the property rental segment which is helping the buy to let market recover gradually. Many brokers are coming back to the market, and are offering reasonable mortgage rates.

Rising demand

Also, the number of people who are looking for properties to rent is increasing by the day. Substandard houses are available on the market, but people are looking for ones with quality. Since quality houses are few in number, there is intense competition, leading to high interest rates. That is why investors are returning once again to the property market to gain from the potentially increasing yields, although some drawbacks still remain.

To describe it numerically, government authorities provided figures in July 2011 that showed a 55% increase in the number of people renting buy to let properties. Between 2003 and 2010, the number of people living in private rented houses grew by £1.25 million. The increase in private property rentals is mostly due to the high housing prices in the UK.

Moreover, the government has failed to provide affordable houses to cater to the needs of the population. In fact, the number of people who are looking for homes has far exceeded the quantity of available property. This also explains why rents have increased in the UK. Plus, since people cannot afford to buy new homes, they will rent houses for longer tenures.

The increase in the number of people who are renting for a longer period, along with high rents has brought about the re-emergence of buy to let investors in the market. According to statistics provided by the CML, lending in the buy to let market has increased by £0.8 billion between 2010 and 2011. Moving on, rental property is also being sought increasingly by university students, both foreign and local. Students who apply to universities in the UK need accommodation nearby, as the universities themselves cannot provide lodgings for everyone. The growth in the number of tenants who are students is therefore another reason why the buy to let market is coming back to its feet.

Recovery takes time

While viewing the data and reading the facts, you must keep in mind that these are baby steps towards recovery. The economy, particularly the residential sector, is still in a crash and it will take some time to turn around.

That is why it was mentioned before that buy to let, at this point in time, should only be considered as a long-term business venture. If you are entering the market for short-term gains, you have to be really careful. The demand for housing is as old as society itself and the value of property will continue to increase in the future. But at the current moment, and in the coming years, there is likely to be a negative growth.

If you plan to invest in buy to let property, be prepared for your capital being tied up for a long time. You would not be able to liquidate your assets easily as that would require evicting your long-term paying guests and selling the property. That is not a simple job.

'Government authorities provided figures in July 2011 that showed a 55% increase in the number of people renting buy to let properties.'

Another factor to be considered here is that even though there is a growing need for rented property, housing prices at the moment are forming a restriction for new investors. Many established owners are already attempting to sell out their property before the value falls, and this will subsequently increase the number of tenants on the market. You will need the advice given in the previous chapter about selecting the right property in order to succeed in this scenario. That is how other successful landlords are managing it.

Do you have what it takes?

To sum it up, *no one* can claim with complete certainty whether the buy to let market will succeed or not. If you are a person who follows opinions and doesn't make personal judgements, then you will always be confused as far as this business is concerned. If you believe in the stars and luck, even they cannot help you. Always repeat the question 'do I have what it takes?' as that will determine your plan of action.

'*No one* can claim with complete certainty whether the buy to let market will succeed or not.'

You require creativity and ingenuity to make profits in today's market. Be willing to try out new ideas if the conventional ones no longer reap the benefits. Look for new ways to obtain your capital and generate an income. The best option is to seek the advice of successful buy to let landlords. Merely reading information and analysing statistics is not enough. The only way to learn is through experience. Without making an attempt, you will never be able to earn profits from investing in property, nor realise the potentials of buy to let investments.

Benefits of renting houses

You can treat your property as stock. You buy it, wait for the prices to go high, and then sell it for a profit. Although this is a good method of accumulating wealth, it requires a lot of patience as well. You will not be getting any immediate returns, and till the property is sold, you have to spend money to take care of it. Moreover, what if prices do not rise for many years?

That is why putting up the property for rent is a great method of earning a nice income before selling out the house. We have already discussed why the demand for rented houses is rising in the UK, but it will also help people to learn at what levels the benefits of renting houses exceed those of purchasing them. You should know that there is a constant debate going whether people should rent houses or buy them.

To take sides in this debate and reach a conclusion, you have to calculate the purchase of the house and the total rent for one year. If the difference is not too great (about 15% or less), then it would actually benefit you to make the purchase instead of renting.

However, if the difference is greater (20% or more), then you would be at a disadvantage by purchasing the house. You should know that additional costs are also there, such as taxes and maintenance, raising the total bill by a significant amount. It also depends whether you are paying the full price at purchase or using a mortgage. It would not be wise to purchase a property whose mortgage payment is higher than the monthly rent.

'In most places in the UK, you will find that the difference between the price of the house and the rent favours renting the property.'

In most places in the UK, you will find that the difference between the price of the house and the rent favours renting the property. Although one can argue that even though mortgage payments are higher than the rent, purchasing the property ultimately can help to make gains in the long run in terms of wealth accumulation. In the past four decades, trends have shown that ownership as compared to tenancy has helped to make wealth accumulation a reality.

However, people who became wealthy while renting property were not entirely absent from the trends. Since it is believed traditionally that having one's own house is better than renting, many people do not consider renting houses as a viable option. But in recent times, especially in the last decade, people are increasingly changing this trend.

How does renting a property help in wealth accumulation?

There are two aspects involved. Firstly, when there is a significant gap between the rent and the mortgage payment, you can rent the house and use the extra money to invest in stocks and bonds, or simply deposit it in the bank to earn interest. Secondly, when you personally own a property, you have to pay money to take care of the property, along with the taxes and mortgages.

This means that there is a notable cash outflow as well. When you live in the house as a tenant, you will also have to spend money on monthly payments, but usually, outflow is greater if you purchase the building. In the long run, as money comes in from your extra investment, as less money goes out on mortgages, you will mount up an impressive amount of wealth. If people think about renting properties in this way, along with their necessity, then the demand for rented houses will increase even further, helping the buy to let market become stronger.

There are no excuses

Another great reason for buying to let is that there are virtually no excuses for not doing so. Many people complain that buying to let, and perhaps all business ventures, consume a lot of time that they are already running short of. To begin with, who has time nowadays? Secondly, can you think of any important financial activity that does *not* require time?

'Your ability to make accurate forecasts based on proper research can determine to a great extent the kind of cash flow you will have.'

The issue is basically of time management. If you can prioritise your tasks and strive to do more productive work, then you will realise that time is not an issue at all. The other excuse that people make has to do with money. Once again, is there any profitable venture that you can do without spending any money? That is why we mentioned the importance of creativity and ingenuity.

You can always find reliable ways of obtaining finance, and you can always get deals on mortgages. Not to mention, it just takes a little extra time to find a property that is sure to attract tenants. Therefore, this excuse is also not valid. What about cash flow issues? Most people are concerned about the high cash outflow buy to let landlords face that ultimately causes them to lose the property.

But you must realise that cash flow depends on a lot of factors. Particularly, your ability to make accurate forecasts based on proper research can determine to a great extent the kind of cash flow you will have. You can always consult professionals and other successful landlords for advice on these matters. But be careful who you consult, as there are lot of inexperienced agents as well. If you cannot carry out these tasks, then don't blame the market for your loss.

Another factor that people use as an excuse is the risk involved in buy to let investments. For the last time, is there any . . . ? I do not need to complete the question as you probably would have recognised what is being implied here. All investments have some risks, but that simply does not mean that no returns are achieved. It is annoying when people look at something inherent in the system and use it as an excuse to reject the whole thing.

To balance the argument of risks, think of all the gains that can be achieved. You will earn rent anyway, but selling out your property when prices rise can make you rich. Will you look at the reward or will you focus on the risk? There is a very thin line between optimism and pessimism. Which side of the line are you standing on?

Finally, most people hesitate to even think about buying to let because they do not know where to start. Being afraid to take the first step is not a unique problem as everyone faces this fear. However, where would this world be if people did not take the first step out of fear? Think about it. This book was written for this reason as well, i.e. to help you take your first step.

Buy to let hotel rooms

If buy to let was a new term for you, then buy to let hotel rooms will also be an unfamiliar concept. The principle is the same. You buy property to earn monthly income. But this time, you purchase rooms in hotels through which you earn a yearly income. Although it is not known popularly, buy to let hotel rooms is taking root as viable option for property investment.

There are a lot of benefits of investing in buy to let hotel rooms. Firstly, purchasing a hotel room runs low risks as compared to investment in property. Although you have only paid for one or more rooms, the success depends on the brand name and quality of the hotel. Also, you do not receive direct income from the room fees, but since these rooms are purchased together, the owners earn a profit.

If you compare this with a buy to let property, that house may be empty for long periods of time without generating any income. Therefore, you are likely to incur a loss. But hotel rooms are in demand all year round, providing greater

'Will you look at the reward or will you focus on the risk? There is a very thin line between optimism and pessimism. Which side of the line are you standing on?'

security of income. Secondly, purchasing hotels to let requires low start-up capital compared to buying property. As we have mentioned before, although the market is growing again, it is still not easy to find buy to let house finance.

When you purchase hotel rooms, you have expert managers and agents, even abroad, to help you arrange the finance and provide you with the best deals. Banks also do not hesitate to provide finance to these types of ventures as their risk is low and the returns are fairly good. If you are finding it difficult to obtain finances for purchasing property, then consider investing in hotel rooms.

Thirdly, when you invest in buy to let hotel rooms, you not only benefit from regular income, but you also have at your disposal, greater prospects of increasing it. It is a known fact that during busy seasons, your rooms can go for double the price. Plus, you will automatically reap the benefits of the growth of the hotel itself.

'When you invest in buy to let hotel rooms, you not only benefit from regular income, but you also have at your disposal, greater prospects of increasing it.'

Furthermore, one of the greatest benefits of investing in buy to let hotel rooms is that someone else takes care of the maintenance of the room. The professional and experienced staff of the hotel will not only take care of the repairs and cleaning, but they will also decorate and upgrade the room from time to time. This is entirely different from the letting agents that landlords hire, because at the hotel, you do not have to pay extra for these services.

You will not have to handle tenant complaints if you invest in hotel rooms, where customer issues will be dealt by the people at the hotel while you relax, even in another city or country! If you want to earn a regular income without any day-to-day hassle, this option is just for you!

Finally, since you own the room(s) yourself, you can always put it to private use at any time of the year. You will be at the disadvantage of not finding hotel rooms at peak times, but you will not have to pay any charges either.

Overseas properties

Remember, although buying to let is usually considered an option for investing in local property, there are great prospects of investing in foreign markets as well. In fact, many buyers who've taken this line of investment have experienced great short-term returns. The buy to let market has improved even in the international sphere, and the tourism industry is the main force behind this growth.

The option of owning a property overseas without additional costs and legal requirements has allowed investing in holiday homes to become a market of its own in recent years. You can also develop a good reputation as a property landlord. The best part is that investing overseas will save you from all the hassles of maintaining a second home. You will not have to look after it, and there are excellent options to choose these services in the other country.

This is a great way to earn a steady income without having to deal with the day-to-day issues of keeping the property. You can hire professionals to take care of your property, promote your house to potential tenants, and even pay and receive all the necessary bills on your behalf. Many overseas property developers offer great packages that include attractive prices, guaranteed rental income, and completely furnished buildings. All these factors further encourage investors to use their money in foreign markets as well.

There has also been significant growth in the tourism and holiday sector. Cheaper transportation has also attracted many people to seek out holiday opportunities in foreign countries, which is why investing in property in these places is profitable. Location, once again, is the key. Only then can you charge desirable rent. You may well know that the rental returns will not be consistent all year round. That is why you should strive for maximum returns by setting up a practical rental yield.

Location

As far as the location is concerned, the resort style tourist spots are really famous. If it is near the airport, accessible to amenities and has a good road and transport system, then the high rents can be charged easily. When you are purchasing a resort (be it a beach or ski resort), estimate the time period in which the greatest number of tourists are likely to rent it. For example, a ski resort is likely to be used for only two months, while the rest of the season it will either be empty, or occupied by the owner. This will not generate the profits you are striving for.

You can even invest in resorts in the coastal area, and further inside the city. These properties can be used for short-term rentals in tourist seasons, while the rest of the year they can be let out on a long-term basis. Country homes or farm houses are also viable options, but the returns on these properties is highly dependent on the level of remoteness, as well their proximity to necessary facilities.

Other benefits

The emergence of buying to let internationally has led to greater economic co-operation between governments that encourage foreign investment into their country. That is why it is highly possible that you can even get tax returns on your overseas house. Plus, you can always spend your holidays in your own property!

Summing Up

- Investing in the buy to let market should not be seen as a get rich quick scheme, but should be viewed as a long-term investment.

- Lending in the buy to let market has increased in recent years due to a number of factors, such as a rise in the number of people renting properties for longer periods of time, and a growth in the number of tenants who are students or young people who are unable to afford to buy their own home.

- One of the main benefits of investing in property is it can be treated as stock. It is bought, kept while waiting for prices to rise, then sold for a profit. Renting it out in the meantime ensures a regular income is earned also.

- If you are effective in time management, able to obtain the necessary finance and conduct the appropriate research, there is no reason why you shouldn't be successful in the buy to let market.

- Buy to let hotel rooms are becoming increasingly popular as an option for property investment. In comparison with general buy to let residential properties, there are a number of advantages of renting out hotel rooms, such as the year round demand that means you are less likely to suffer from loss of income due to an empty property.

Chapter Four

Tax Implications

No one likes to think about taxes. But unfortunately you cannot avoid them, especially when you are in the letting business. The regulations are lengthy and detailed. Plus they change from time to time. We will guide you in the tax implications of buying to let, but it will always be better for you to consult a tax specialist or an accountant when you are actually doing the business.

The two taxes

When you invest in buy to let, you will have to pay two main types of taxes called income tax and capital gains tax. Income tax will be charged on your net income at the highest marginal rate. The rent will be your income in this case, and you can fall in a basic, or even a high tax bracket. The highest rate can go up to 40%.

The largest payment that will be deducted from your gross income is likely to be the mortgage payment. Please note that your capital *repayment* will not be deducted by tax. You will also be allowed maintenance and repairs costs in this tax bracket (more on this to follow). It is, therefore, more cost effective (as far as tax is concerned) to have a mortgage on a buy to let property than your own home. You should also hire an accountant to help you seek the tax breaks you need.

A capital gains tax, on the other hand, is levied on the profit you make while selling your buy to let house. The capital gains tax will be only charged on the property that you have invested in, and not your own residence. If one property is serving both purposes, then the tax will be apportioned accordingly. This tax will be calculated in line with the retail price index to cover the effects of inflation. Since this tax is not levied on a private residence, couples who live apart will have *both* their homes exempt. There are also some tax reliefs, which will be discussed later.

Capital gains tax rate was 18% back in 2008. But, as of 2010, gains above a fixed amount (£10,100) will be subject to this tax. You also have to pay stamp duty on your buy to let property. As of 2011, stamp duty rates are:

- 1% on £125,000 and above.
- 3% on £250,000 and above.
- 4% on £500,000 and above.

At the current time, properties that are under £175,000 have a stamp duty holiday until the year end.

'You should always seek expert help when it comes to taxes.'

Many buy to let owners, especially the experienced ones, try to avoid paying taxes. One of the most common methods to do this is to put the other property (the one for letting) in the name of a partner. Since the partner will be 'living' there, no capital gain will be charged if the property is to be sold.

However, this does not only violate the law, but also the rules of lending and borrowing. Your finance could be ceased, along with legal punishments like fines and imprisonment. There are other methods of reducing tax payments as well, but these are often too complicated for new landlords. For example, setting up a company to own the properties is an effective way of lowering tax rates, but a new investor cannot afford it. Coming back full circle to the first point, you should always seek expert help when it comes to taxes.

Buy to let income tax

To put it in simple terms, income tax will be charged on your rent earnings, just like a tax on any other source of earnings like salary, wages, etc. If, for example, you fall in the 20% tax bracket, this percentage would be deducted from the total rent you received in the year. You can, as mentioned before, be pushed up to the 40% bracket if you have additional earnings that make your total income £37,401 or more.

Also, remember that not all of the rent you earn will be subject to taxation. Some expenses and payments will be deducted from the gross rent income before tax is calculated from the net amount. This is a general description, let's move on to the details.

Basically there are two sources of income if you are a buy to let landlord. Not only do you receive the rent, but the tenants also have to pay you a deposit at the beginning of their renting period. Moreover, the rate of the tax is determined by the amount that the tenant still owes in the tax year instead of the actual rent received throughout. So if, for example, you are paid in advance, only the amount that comes under the tax period will be levied, the remaining amount being taxed in the next tax year.

On the other hand, if the tenant does not pay in time, the amount that is accrued will still be taxed if it falls in the tax season. Only if the tenant declares that he/she cannot pay the amount owed, will you not be taxed on that sum. Deposits usually are not subject to taxation, as you have to repay them to the tenant. However, in the case of significant damage done to the property by the tenant, the landlord has the right to cease the payment, or withhold some portion of the amount him/herself. The amount in this case will be subject to taxation.

Of course, as mentioned before, there will be various costs that you will have to pay in order to maintain the property. Some of these are allowed expenses, which means that they are not included in the tax. These expenses include:

- Repair costs.
- General maintenance expenses.
- Cost of providing utilities and other services.
- Interest payments on the amount of the loan.
- Insurance on the building or any object within the property.
- Payments to letting agencies.
- Payments made to accountants.
- 10% for furniture replacement in a furnished buy to let.

There are also some unavoidable expenses as well, the ones that will not be counterbalanced from your income. Some of these costs include:

■ Costs of sale and purchase of the building.

■ Repayments of the loan/mortgage.

■ Costs that you have to bear while the property is still empty.

■ Costs of renovation.

■ Costs incurred while improving the house or increasing its value.

If a cost is not offset against your rental income, you can be relieved of the expense. However, it will fall in your capital tax gain if you plan to sell out the property. Please remember that this information is not meant to be a detailed guide to the property tax laws of the UK; we have just provided a structure of how this system works, and which amount will be deducted as tax from your income as landlord. For a furnished letting, the laws pertaining to income tax are totally different as we will explain later.

'If a cost is not offset against your rental income, you can be relieved of the expense. However, it will fall in your capital tax gain if you plan to sell out the property.'

Capital gains tax

When you sell your buy to let property, the amount that you gain from the selling price (which is higher than the price you bought it for) is subject to the capital gains tax. Some of the costs that will be included in this tax are:

■ Expenses incurred during the sale and purchase of the house.

■ Legal costs.

■ Fees paid to estate agents.

■ Stamp duty.

You may not be given any tax relief on your income tax when you carry out renovations to the house or improve the property in any way. However, you may be able to avoid the inclusion of these expenses in your capital gains tax when you finally sell your property. The sum total that you will actually pay in tax will be for the duration of your ownership, or if you have lived in the house yourself any time.

Capital gains tax causes the greatest amount of anxiety among property owners. In the tax year 2009-2010, £9,600 was the allowable personal gain amount that was not subject to taxation. This was also true if the property was owned by two partners, and each got a tax exemption of £9,600. If you make profits more than this amount, then capital gains tax would be levied anywhere between 10%-40%.

Owning a second property

The people who fear this tax more than others are the ones who own a second property as well. Individual residential buildings are not subject to this tax, but officers are always on the hunt for people who have a second home! People are discouraged if their second home, or in this case, a buy to let property is heavily taxed.

Everyone's main residence is exempt from tax, and it is known as the principle private residence. However, you can also get a reduction in your tax bills on your second property. This is done by living in that house for a limited amount of time. Houses that serve as the main dwelling will be tax exempt for the period in which you lived there, plus the final three years of possession. So all the while you rent the property and live there, you will not have to pay the capital gains tax when you sell the house.

When you buy a second property, you will be given two years to declare which one of the properties is your main home. Of course, for this period, you do not have to live in the house necessarily. If, however, due to certain reasons the owner fails to choose one property as the central residence, then they would have to prove which house they were living in to make it not liable for capital gains tax.

Do not forget about this two year period to gain some relief from taxation. If you do so, you can always get an additional period if you purchase yet another house, your third property. The period can also be extended if your second house becomes your principle residence. In order to prove that the second home is the principle residence, you have to:

- Transfer your bank details.

- Change your postal address.

'In the tax year 2009-2010, £9,600 was the allowable personal gain amount that was not subject to taxation.'

- Change the details for the election of the main home.

This information will help you prove that you were living in the second house, or even renting it. If you (or your partner) have rented your own house in the past, you can gain from the letting reliefs up to £40,000. If a married couple owns the property together, then each partner can realise the benefits and increase the amount of tax relief. However, individual tax relief will not be greater than the amount mentioned before.

Another way to lower the tax bills is by transferring the incidence of taxation onto the partner with the lowest tax rate. However, this option is only for married people. Sounds easy? But things are not as clear as they appear when you read this information. Never try to evade taxes illegally, and when faced with the smallest complication or confusion, seek the help of financial experts.

'Never try to evade taxes illegally, and when faced with the smallest complication or confusion, seek the help of financial experts.'

Furnished holiday lettings tax

Owners of a furnished holiday letting, or a holiday home can benefit from some tax advantages, only if the property meets some specific guidelines. Firstly, your property must be within the UK. It should be well furnished, and must be open for commercial holiday letting for the general public for about 150 days, and it should be actually rented for at least half of these days.

You should offer no discounts and cheaper rates, even to friends and family, and only charge the fee based on the market rate. Another rule for tax benefits is that you should let your holiday period for a short period, almost a month. If your furnished holiday property qualifies, you can receive capital allowances. You will also be able to gain some exemption from the capital gains tax when you sell the house.

If, on the other hand, the holiday home does not comply to the taxation rules, the taxes will be levied in the same way as a buy to let home. As far as the calculations of the tax are concerned, they will be carried out in the same way as any other rental income. However, there is a slight difference. Whereas the cost of maintenance and repair (wear and tear) will be allowable on the rental income, you will be given capital allowances on your holiday lettings.

For example, the cost of purchasing and maintaining furnishings and furniture, along with costs of heavy equipment like refrigerators, air conditioners and washing machines will come under capital allowances in your holiday furnishing let. If you incur a loss on your furnished property, you can always carry it forward and counterbalance with future profits. However, you can use a loss to lower your income that is to be taxed.

You can even delay the payment of the capital gains tax on a holiday let if you invest the gains you made with it in three in other businesses. In this way, you can delay the payment of the capital gains tax till you sell off the other businesses or assets as well. Just like your earnings and expenses, you need to declare the income you generated from the holiday letting on the annual self-assessment tax return.

It is also helpful if you maintain the proper paperwork throughout the year. Document the following things:

- The total amount of rent you received during the year.

- The dates at which you received the rent.

- The expenses you incurred on the property.

- Bank statements, invoices and receipts.

Rent a room scheme

The rent a room scheme is earning rent by letting only one furnished room in your property. You can earn more than £4,000 in a year without paying tax. Of course, the amount will be divided if you have a partner. This is a great scheme for earning income that is tax exempt by making one room in your main house (if you have other properties) or your only house, available for tenants.

Apart from your expenses, no amount of your earnings from letting rooms will be taxed. Even if you are earning from other venues, you will still be exempt from taxes in a rent a room scheme. You can easily benefit from this scheme by furnishing any of the rooms in your house and allowing a paying guest to lodge in. You can even let an entire floor of the building.

This is not similar to renting out flats and apartments. That is not classified as rent a room. The scheme is also not applicable if the room you are letting is not furnished. It is not necessary that you own the home. However, if you are renting the place yourself, or paying mortgage payments, check the regulations to see whether they stipulate this scheme or not.

As mentioned before, if the house is owned by two partners, both will receive half the earnings. Currently, the amount is £4,250 for a single owner. You can charge extra rates for providing services like meals, cleaning and laundry. However, you need to add this income to the total rent as well and report it to the tax authority. You will be taxed on income more than £4,250, even if the rent is less than the amount.

Along with the benefits, there are some drawbacks of this scheme as well. For example, there are no allowable expenses that you can claim, even of maintenance, repairs, utilities and insurance. Even losses cannot be claimed. Moreover, if you do not go for this scheme, you will pay income tax on rent received. On the other hand, even if you do let a room, the additional income, over £4,250, will be taxed. To make your decision, you need to calculate two things.

Firstly, calculate the income that you will be left with after paying all the expenses, which will be your profit. Secondly, work out the additional earnings over £4,250 you can make by providing extra services. This system can also be converted into a single room bread and breakfast business. All you have to do is to mention the type of business on your self-assessment tax return.

If you wish to pursue this mode of letting property, tax exemption is automatic if the income is under the tax-free threshold. If, on the other hand, your receipts are above the exemption range, you need to file and report it. If you do not want to avail this scheme, you have to state your rental income and expenses for the tax year. Finally, whichever option you choose, it is still worthwhile to keep a set of records for future convenience, in case you decide to join or quit this scheme.

Summing Up

- There are two main taxes that are charged on buy to let properties: income tax and capital gains tax.

- Income tax is charged on your net income (i.e. the rent you receive) at the highest marginal rate, which in some cases can be up to 40%.

- Capital gains tax is levied on any profit made from the sale of a buy to let property, but is only charged on this property if it is not cited as the owner's principle residence.

- Stamp duty is also charged on buy to let properties at varying rates depending on value.

- Holiday lettings and the rent a room scheme are two additional means of earning income from letting, both of which have taxation laws associated with them.

- There are various ways of reducing tax bills and claiming reliefs that help to lower tax. To ensure you receive the full benefits of these and comply with all UK tax laws, it is advised you enlist the services of a qualified expert.

Chapter Five

Getting Properties Insured

Protecting your investment

If you have properties, especially ones for letting out to tenants, then you need to protect them at all costs. That is why you should get your buy to let house insured. Your policy will serve as a contingency plan in times of damage caused by water, fire, nature, etc. Not only is this a back-up plan, but it is also an important responsibility for the landlord, because the property is not only for his/her personal use; strangers live in it as well, and there are potential dangers involved.

Your normal housing insurance does not offer coverage on accidents or thefts in your rental house and you would not be reimbursed with this kind of insurance plan, unlike a landlord's policy. This type of policy stipulates that the owner of the house must carry out safety checks on the gas and electrical equipment, wiring and piping. After these checks, a typical landlord's policy will help you cover:

* Pest control and rats.
* Water damage.
* Home repairs.
* Concrete damages.

Although these things look like routine occurrences, they do need insurance coverage. That is why you should go for the most comprehensive policy that you can. Another factor to consider is that the sole reason you invested in the

'Your normal housing insurance does not offer coverage on accidents or thefts in your rental house.'

property was to attract tenants and generate rental income. But what will you do if there are no tenants? Therefore, you will require an insurance policy that covers this eventuality.

Moreover, if there are bad tenants who do not pay you at all and you are without any insurance policy to cover the expenses, you are left in an adverse position financially. For these reasons and more, a buy to let business plan is simply incomplete without an insurance plan.

Is it important?

If you have decided to become a buy to let landlord, you will have to choose a good insurance policy. You may have been offered one already, but you need to do some research before selecting what is best for you. Insurance policies for buy to let landlords are specifically known as landlord insurance, as they are specifically designed for property owners.

What is covered?

Just like a typical insurance policy, the terms and conditions cover information varying from person to person. However, some factors are common to all buy to let landlord policies.

Damage to property

Firstly, a landlord's policy will cover serious damages to the building itself from natural disasters and accidents like fire, flooding, electricity, explosion, etc. This is just like a regular housing policy. However, a landlord's policy will also cover the damage caused by the paying residents of the house. Some of these damages include:

- Damage to the walls.
- Broken windows.
- Holes drilled or nails in the walls or the ceiling.

Misuse of the inventory will also be covered in a landlord's insurance plan. This is known as the contents cover. Damage done to any of the materials provided by the landlord inside the rental property will be reimbursed. This includes things like furniture, carpets, curtains and furnishings. Any breakage, loss or theft will be covered.

Other features will be different as you view policies offered by different companies. You can decide what to include. Do a lot of brainstorming to determine the things you need to cover in your insurance policy, because there are a lot of risks involved when you are a buy to let landlord. For example, there is a chance that your tenant may die in the rental property. This is not unlikely at all.

Electrocutions, gas leakage, poisoning, falling walls and ceilings do not happen all the time, but they do happen. You need to include public liability cover in your insurance policy to cover such mishaps. You may need to pay relatives of anyone deceased as a result of an incident/accident in the property, who may want to claim a settlement.

Loss of rent

Another risk that you may have to face is the loss of rent. This is not as unfortunate as death, but it is still likely to happen. Assume that there is an accident like a fire that destroys your property and you have to move your tenants for some time. You will not only lose the rent at this time, but you will also have to pay the relocation expenses.

By including the loss of rent option in your landlord insurance policy, you will effectively cover these costs. Some good policies can cover almost 36 months while the damage is being dealt with. You may want every aspect of your property letting to be covered by insurance, but that is next to impossible. However, a good policy will give you far more benefits than a regular housing insurance cover.

Who's not covered?

You should be aware that there are some insurance policies that do not cover all kinds of tenants. These include:

'Misuse of the inventory will also be covered in a landlord's insurance plan. This is known as the contents cover.'

- Students.
- Immigrants.
- Social security tenants.

If you do not plan to let your property to such tenants and only allow professionals to live your house, then you will not have a problem. However, if your house is available on rent for all kinds of people, you may want to find an insurance policy that is not person specific.

Legal costs

'It is highly possible that your mortgage lender may demand that you have an insurance policy in order to get the finance.'

Finally, all tenures do not start and finish as smoothly as you want them to. There can be trouble with the tenants, and there could also be issues regarding eviction. You would need to file a case in the county court to force the tenants to leave your property. The legal costs involved in such matters are huge, and you should go for a policy that covers such expenses.

You may not consider a policy for this as necessary, but it is better than coming out of these issues without any money left in your pocket! It is highly possible that your mortgage lender may demand that you have an insurance policy in order to get the finance. But even if that is not the case, you should consider a landlord insurance policy seriously. Property investment is an important, once in a lifetime decision. Therefore, insurance is vital to protect your investment.

Selecting the best policy for you

A good buy to let insurance policy will cover property damage, loss of rent and legal fees. As mentioned before, choosing a policy is not a legal requirement for a landlord and, therefore, is not compulsory. However, having a policy does prove beneficial in the future. Certainly, it is better than paying damages from your own pocket for accidents that you didn't cause!

Landlord policies are available widely nowadays, and that is why you have to do some thinking before selecting the right one. Insurance policies, even those of a landlord, are similar in the basic content. They cover things like:

- Building repairs.

- Replacement costs.
- Delayed or no rent payments.
- Legal costs.

The details will differ, and they also influence the cost of the policy. One policy may give you rent cover for up to a year, yet another might give you the same option for a longer period of time. Likewise, an insurance provider may only cover your rent payments up to 15% of the total amount, while another policy covers 20% of your rent repayments.

Some insurance policies you will see provide payments for the relocation of tenants when the property gets damaged and is no longer fit to live in, yet others do not have this option at all. Another twist in the details can happen like this: a policy will cover the relocation costs, but it may deduct from the amount apportioned for the loss of rent. Yet it is also possible to find a policy that offers both options without any deductions!

It is options like these that will make some policies worth choosing while you simply pass over the others. The choice will also depend on your personal preferences, as well as the kind of tenants you are looking for. That is why you should go through a number of options and make written comparisons of the details that you may find worth noting. You should also remember, as we mentioned before, that some policies do specify the type of tenants they will cover. You target market should be really clear in your mind even while choosing the insurance policy.

Remember, it is really important to choose a good landlord insurance policy. You can get a property contents insurance cover by paying £10 per month to take care of any unforseen mishaps. A more complete landlord insurance policy which considers the greatest numbers of risks on a buy to let investment can be bought for up to £40 per month. The cost also depends on the value of the house, as well as the terms and conditions laid down in the policy.

This may seem costly to you, but it is still far better than not having any insurance at all. All you have to do is take some extra time and do some research on your own. You can also consult someone who is experienced in this field and someone who you trust. This way you can be sure to select the best insurance policy.

'Remember, it is really important to choose a good landlord insurance policy.'

How to find an insurance policy

To save some time, you can search for insurance policies over the Internet. By comparing different landlord policies over the Internet, you can easily find one that suits your needs. Advances in technology, as well as in the buy to let industry, have not only enabled property owners to find insurance policies online, but to purchase them as well.

This is also a great way of staying up to date on the latest information about the market, especially with regards to insurance. Buying insurance online is simply a grand option of saving time to attend to other responsibilities that a landlord has. When you are looking for different policies, you should firstly consider the coverage that each policy offers. When you look for quotes online, you will be in a better position to differentiate between the various offers and their pros and cons.

Coverage is perhaps even more important than the cost of the policy itself. And this is not only true for new landlords, but also for established property owners who want to keep their policies updated and look for new ones that provide better coverage. A clear comparison of landlord insurance policies will help an experienced landlord review his/her present policy and compare it with the new ones on the market. It is a fact that instead of renewing an old policy, purchasing a new one altogether has proven far more economic to landlords.

It is easy to understand why anyone would look for a policy at reasonable rates and good coverage. Buy to let is a business after all, and the essence of any business is to cut down all possible costs to earn all possible profits. It is only by comparison that you can find the right policy that helps you financially. Apart from the coverage, the price of the policy also matters. Search the new products available on the market, and compare them with any policy that you have been offered in the past.

The dynamics of the buy to let industry can also help you to get a good insurance policy at competitive rates. This is smart decision, one with great monetary benefits. You may have inhibitions about the effort and paperwork involved, or you may be simply lazy and go for the first policy that you come across, only for the sake of doing it. But this is not an (economically) healthy attitude. The difference of even a few pounds can have long-term effects. That is why it is better to be wise because the effort is worth it.

How to get a reasonable policy

Estimations

To begin with, you have to calculate the value of your building, as well as the contents or the inventory inside it. Of course, these calculations will not be 100% accurate as they are estimations. But these estimations are necessary, as the quote you will receive from the insurance company will depend on these valuations. Another amount that needs to be estimated is the cost of repairs or rebuilding should the property be damaged.

This kind of property check will be carried out by specialists, who will provide a written report of their findings. The most inexpensive policies will not provide coverage for significant damages. Hence, you have to be really careful to maintain the balance between price and coverage.

Quotes

Next you will have to go through all the quotes that you receive. Think your way through when you are picking and choosing prices from various companies as quotes vary for different types of houses. Be clear about this factor with your insurance provider to receive quotes that are appropriate for your property, as quotes are different for normal houses and commercial properties. Describe the kind of building you have, and even the business operations you plan to carry out in it. Also be honest about its condition while communicating with the agent. In this way, you will receive quotes according to the requirements of the building.

Comparing the coverage

This point has been already noted before. While viewing the various quotes that are offered to you, go through the various coverage options as carefully as possible. Also get all the relevant information about the recent offers on the market. Most of these policies are economical and provide great coverage

'The dynamics of the buy to let industry can also help you to get a good insurance policy at competitive rates.'

options to the landlord. Comparison will also help you find the right company to deal with, and that could change into a long-term relationship for your continual insurance needs.

How to keep the premium low

If you only have one property, then insurance premiums may not form a significant portion of your expenses. However, this is not the same for property owners who maintain a portfolio of different buildings. One property or many, you can always use some effective methods to keep your premiums low so that you can gain the maximum benefit from your insurance policies.

Single policy

Firstly, if you maintain a portfolio, try to cover all the buildings in a single insurance policy. This will help you in many ways. You will be able to avoid confusion about the dates of renewal if you have a single policy. Plus, there is something known as bulk discount. Getting more than one building insured will definitely entitle you to discounts from a good insurance company.

Choose the 'right' tenants

Another way to lower your insurance premium is to hire the right kind of tenants. There are always some bad ones who give you trouble, not only in terms of delayed or no rent payments, but also in terms of property damage. The best people to let out your property to are professionals with steady jobs. Not only do they provide a greater assurance of timely payments, but letting out to them will also help you lower the premium as risks are low.

Play it safe

You can reduce your premium by employing safety measures in your property. Just by installing good security alarms, you can save up to 10% on your insurance premium. You should also think about including a landlord emergency cover in your insurance policy. Although this may add to your monthly payments, you will be relieved of spending your money and effort on a callout when any mishap occurs.

Finally, it is true that potential risks cannot be given an accurate monetary value, but you should try to be as shrewd as possible while making estimations of any likely hazards. Being uninsured to save money is not a good option under any circumstance, but paying for coverage you do not need is also something to be avoided.

'By installing good security alarms, you can save up to 10% on your insurance premium.'

Summing Up

* If you purchase a buy to let property you should protect this investment by taking out an effective insurance policy, ensuring it covers all expenditures and eventualities you, as owner, are liable and responsible for.

* Insurance policies for buy to let properties differ significantly in detail from normal household policies.

* In-depth research to find the best and most suitable landlord insurance can be carried out on the Internet. If you are confident to go ahead without advice from a professional, you can also purchase insurance online too.

* There are a number of ways a landlord can save money and keep premiums low, including buying a single policy to cover all buildings, employing effective safety measures (e.g. installing burglar alarms) and choosing the 'right' sort of tenants.

Chapter Six

Potential Pitfalls and How to Avoid Them

Overview

We have mentioned previously that the current market conditions have left many people wondering whether buying to let is a good investment option or not. But we concluded that there is no harm in stepping into the market at this time. Many people consider this a great time for investing in property and some of them have done it already, owing to the hope that both the housing industry as well as the economy will come to their feet again.

You also know by now that just like all businesses, there are some potential risks and pitfalls involved in buying to let. These risks are covered with a widespread negativity about this industry. However, property owners who have acted wisely and have entered the market fully prepared have made an impressive income from buy to let properties.

This means that this market is only for those people who have foresight, and who plan ahead to avoid all the possible pitfalls. You should be realistic while estimating your current financial position, how much finance you can obtain, and whether you have the ability to spend a great deal of time in finding and convincing your first tenants. It is highly recommended that if you do not have the ample financial resources needed for buying to let, you should wait and take a step back.

It is also true, however, that the present market is the best to make an investment, and many people will need a lot of willpower to hold back! You may face a dilemma, but do not fail to use your brain. Another thing you need

'Property owners who have acted wisely and have entered the market fully prepared have made an impressive income from buy to let properties.'

to remember is that if you purchase property that needs serious repairs, you will need additional capital apart from the mortgage and this will only worsen your financial situation.

We once again remind you to carry out thorough market research to dig out the best deals possible. It is also recommended that you step out of your own locality and look in other areas that are not so far away from your principle residence. Maybe you will find better opportunities there. There has to be balance between the amount you are willing to invest and the estimated rental income that you will be able to earn. And this balance depends on how ripe the market for rented houses is. Always remember that.

Then there is the timeless fact that experts know best. Consulting your financial specialists in a matter can help you decide which area provides the best rental yields. You should also have fellowship with other landlords. New ones can boost your morale, while the experienced ones can provide expert tips and tricks. This may not be easy, however, since no one wants to give away business secrets. You will require good communication skills to accomplish this. Once again, purchase a property that you would be comfortable living in.

What else do you need to remember? Oh yes, anticipate all the probable losses while preparing your estimates. Always keep a certain amount of time (let's say two months) in which you will *not* receive rent, and keep the estimated costs of repairs and maintenance fixed throughout the year. These factors can make or break your budget for the year, so do not forget to consider them.

Not as simple as it seems

To sum it up, *reading* about buying to let makes it look pretty straightforward. You apply for a mortgage and receive it. You then find a suitable property and purchase it. After working on repairs and home improvement, you advertise the house, most probably via a letting or estate agency. Tenants show up and you carry out the necessary checks. After selecting the proper tenants, you draw up the agreement, and hand them the keys.

In reality, things do not run as smoothly as this. To be realistic, buy to let is just like a sport where you are in a hit or miss position, and that will determine whether you win or lose the game.

Some potential drawbacks

In the past few years, the buy to let market has performed really well. While the stock market crashed, house prices sky rocketed. That is why many people are considering buying to let investment as a viable business venture. But that does not mean that simply any investment on any property will succeed. Market research and the ability to handle credit crunches is the key here.

Firstly, anyone who wants to consider buy to let as a set-up for earning regular income must be prepared to be in it for the long run. Rental yield should be the focus here, while wealth accumulation through capital appreciation must be considered a bonus.

Off plan buildings

When you are dealing in buy to let properties, you will encounter something known as off plan buildings. These are buildings that are still under construction, and people purchase them in advance. Until recently, this was seen as a good and easy way to find houses for letting. One significant benefit of purchasing these properties is that till the time they are built, house prices *are* likely to increase, which will help you make greater returns on investment.

However, things are not that easy. On the contrary, off plan investments are observed to end up in a loss as well. Why is that so? Simply because there is a horde of buy to let investors out there in the market who are in a constant hunt for these properties. When these buildings are complete and appear on the market, the increasing numbers of investors end up bringing down rental yields.

Another problem is that developers of such properties use discount offers to lure investors, especially the new ones. What seems a discount is just a fraud most of the time. The discount in reality is often on an exaggerated price. Although such plans have their benefits, the ultimate factor is the rental yield, and how much capital are you able to tie up in the property.

'Anyone who wants to consider buy to let as a set up for earning regular income must be prepared to be in it for the long run.'

Finance and the financer

Usually, finance is a potential pitfall in all businesses and buy to let is no exception. But in this case, even the *financer* can prove to be a pitfall! It is not more difficult to find a mortgage loan in the UK than it is to convince a lender to loan the finance. You can find loans on favourable interest rates, but lenders can act as serious stumbling blocks. They have certain criteria which a landlord has to pass.

For example, you know that a mortgage is based on the income that will be generated by the property, rather than the earnings of the property owner. The estimated rental incomes need to be anywhere between 125%-150% of the amount of the loan, and the yearly rental yield should be around eight percent. Only then can you secure the finance.

Moreover, the landlord who applies for the mortgage must have a principle residence, and he/she must be willing to pay a minimum 15% deposit. Another thing that really makes the lender hesitant is an ex-council property. If, for example, the house is a flat above a store, then the financer can really get uneasy!

That is why it is important to keep your eyes and ears open all the time to get the slightest hint of good property locations. Look at the newspapers every day, and surf the Internet regularly. Although letting agents are really helpful, some of them will show you dreams that cannot be fulfilled. This is especially true when you want to find out the estimated rent you can charge on your property.

You should try to contact an agent as if you were an enquiring tenant, as this will give you a better and maybe a more honest price. Try to find a property close to your main residence. This will not only help you to get first-hand information on the local settings, but you can also manage the property well when you are in close proximity, possibly without hiring a letting agent.

A complete survey of the property is also required, along with decorations, improvements and repairs before the house can be advertised. These things put you in a better bargaining position.

Further drawbacks to avoid

As buying to let is a risky business, there are virtually countless pitfalls at every corner. Here are some more:

Going for every bargain

Landlords really focus on below market value (BMV) properties. However, not all BMV bargains are as promising as they appear to be. In fact, it is highly possible that what looks like a great BMV bargain ends up sucking your resources. Savings are good (as much as £20,000), but if there are any structural issues with the building that were not deducted initially, you may end up spending more than you saved just for fixing the problem. This will create a large depression in your bank balance.

Another issue is that even if the bargain is good and the property has no issues, there is still a chance that no one wants to live there. It may take a long time to find some tenants, and the rent income may not be high enough to make a profit. How can you get around this problem? You should conduct detailed surveys and also keep an eye on the rental market.

'It is highly possibly that what looks like a great BMV bargain ends up sucking your resources.'

Personal preferences

One mistake that most beginners make is that they spend a lot of money on decorating and reshaping the house. Instead of modelling the house in a way in which the tenants can add their own decor, landlords imprint their personal preferences. This is especially true of kitchens and bathrooms, where a lot of money is spent simply because people believe what they like will be appreciated by others as well.

You can easily avoid this problem by preparing a budget before any actual implementation. Estimate the highest amount that can be spent on these activities *without* a burden being placed in the capital. You should further divide this estimate into different areas such as in-house repairs, garden decoration, furnishings, etc. It is easy to get carried away when you look at attractive kitchen and bathroom ware in the market, but you should always focus on the budget.

Inaccurate rental estimations

This one is described as the pit into which you can fall easily, but getting out of it is next to impossible. All too often, new property owners inaccurately make rental estimates in accordance with other properties in the same area. This may work as a research tool in some cases, but it can negatively affect your income. It is highly possible that your property may be in an area that people do not prefer to live in.

'All too often, new property owners inaccurately make rental estimates in accordance with other properties in the same area. This may work as a research tool in some cases, but it can negatively affect your income.'

Moreover, your property may not have the same facilities as another similar house has, which clearly explains the difference in the rent. Unless you have complete information on what each property offers, never make rent comparisons. Be realistic about your own house. As far as determining the rent is concerned, you may have to offer lower rates in the beginning to attract potential tenants. It would be foolish if you let go of some potential residents just because they did not comply with your demand.

This attitude will only prolong the empty period, which should be avoided at all costs. But even when charging a favourable rent, do not keep it *equal* to your costs. Keep it a bit higher, so you may not face negative cash flow if expenses arise. For a better estimate, either visit similar properties to your house on your own, or ask letting agents to view your property and advise what the suitable rent should be. Setting up the rent levels is never easy. Therefore, the advice of professionals really helps.

You should also remember that your aim is to never leave the property vacant and always find tenants to pay your rent on time, so that you will not suffer any losses. But there are many times when property vacancy is unavoidable. For example, your property would remain empty when the present tenants leave and you are waiting to find new ones (or till the new ones move in). Also, during times of repair and renovation, you would have to keep the house empty.

It is also worth noting that rent rates can vary throughout the year and they do not remain consistent. A very good example is the time when summer holidays are about to end. Students who are enrolled in universities need accommodation, so they are in search of rental properties. Furthermore, students who have now graduated and become professionals would also need new houses. Even families with young children who will be joining new schools will require rented houses to settle down. All these factors will make rent rates rise.

Purchasing multiple properties on discount

Many people purchase multiple properties on the same development, or different units in the same building. That is because the developers who build these multi-unit properties offer tempting discounts to lure investors. Once again, although it will save you some money, there is the potential danger that the property does not attract tenants.

This is collective disadvantage (as opposed to collective advantage). You may deem these opportunities great, but only if you know that they will attract tenants should you go ahead. Otherwise, find properties that you know will sell like hot cakes. Remember, there has to be a balance between your investment and expected income.

Ignoring tenant verification

Buy to let investment is useless if you are not able to collect rent from the tenants. There are some tenants who will not pay you. But even the good ones may delay their payments or even default due to a bad credit position. That is why it is compulsory for a landlord to carry out the necessary inspections before letting their house to someone.

Review bank details, ask for references from previous property owners and possibly a written guarantee. This can help you avoid non-payment. If you cannot do this on your own, you can always hire professional letting agents to carry out credit checks and references on your behalf. This may force you to spend extra pounds, but these expenses will pale in comparison to the long-term benefits of adequate research and checks into prospective tenants. You will always have peace of mind as far as the payments are concerned.

'Remember, there has to be a balance between your investment and expected income.'

Moving on

The worst case scenario

As we have illustrated before, those people who are compelled to invest in buying to let just by reading about it have a fairly straightforward conception of what the whole process is going to be like. Optimism is a positive trait, but it should never replace realism. Always consider the worst case scenario when you are doing financial planning and this obviously means that you prepare yourself for times when you will not receive any rent.

'Always consider the worst case scenario when you are doing financial planning and this obviously means that you prepare yourself for times when you will not receive any rent.'

How to reverse this issue? You will have to make good budgets, choose a good property and set a reasonable rental rate. This way you can avoid an empty profit that is making a loss. You should never forget that there are significant costs to bear in addition to mortgage payments when you become a landlord. If you include all these factors in your budget and compare them with the available financial resources, then you will realise yourself whether you have a green light or a stop sign!

Another way to secure payments from the tenants and avoid any bad behaviour is to draw up a tenancy agreement (see chapter 2). This will help you evade the many problems that come with tenancy. Not only will you be able to avoid tenants who will not pay you, but you can also evict them easily if their tenure is clearly specified on a written and signed contract.

It will also specify when the agreement can be renewed. An agent can help you prepare this document.

Tenancy agreements are hugely beneficial, especially for landlords who want to make their properties available for shorter tenancies. These trends are more common in the urban financial centres and metropolitans. The problem is that even though there are shorter tenancies that provide opportunities for greater profits through high rents, there are also significant risks involved.

Dealing with taxes

Tax is a part of our lives and therefore we cannot call it a pitfall as such. However, lack of knowledge regarding tax laws that pertain to property investment can prove to be financially harmful. We have devoted a separate chapter on taxation issues, but let's review some important points.

A buy to let property is considered a business asset. Therefore, you have to pay income tax on your rental earnings. Financial agents recommend that landlords find mortgages on an interest-only loan basis rather than repayment loans. The reason is that all the interest on the loan can be offset against your tax payments. But the selection of the finance depends on how you view your investment.

If you are looking at your buy to let investment as a means of a steady income for a long time, then you should consider paying a larger deposit initially on your mortgage. By doing this, you will be able to reduce the size of these payments on your monthly income. Plus there are other costs that you can counterbalance against tax. As per the tax regulations, any work done on your property that cannot be clearly called an improvement is not taxed.

For example, insurance, garden maintenance, payments to letting agents and managerial costs do not constitute improvements to the property even though they have to be paid in relation to the house. These costs are open for tax relief. Although the furnishing that happens *before* the initial tenants move in cannot be offset against your tax, after this period you will be allowed almost 10% allowance on your annual income for any furnishing you carry out.

Another way to avoid taxation issues is to maintain accurate records of all your rental income in your annual self-assessment tax return. You can then record this in the Land & Property supplementary pages which can be obtained from the tax office. You will also have to pay the capital gains tax when you sell your buy to let house. The tax will be levied on any profits at your highest income level.

You can refer to chapter 4 to learn ways how to lower your capital gains tax bill. Here is an additional point to remember. If you are a buy to let landlord, your rental property will be included in your estate when you die. This can make it subject to inheritance tax as well.

Doing it on your own

Is it possible to carry out all buying to let without using a letting agent? Yes, it would be wrong to say that you cannot do well without an agent. You are not even required by the law to do so. However, agents can help you immensely when it comes to things like writing up the tenancy agreement, carrying out inspections of the prospective tenants and the day-to-day landlord matters.

Only an experienced person can effectively administer these responsibilities, and therefore new landlords should seriously consider hiring an agent to help them out. However, there is no fixed rule book for the practice of agents and there are chances that you will fall prey to frauds. If you want to hire letting agents, you should always go for a member of the ARLA (Association of Residential Letting Agents) as they follow a strict code of ethics.

'Many people do not realise that managing property is more expensive than obtaining and repaying the mortgage!'

A good agent will help you find tenants and help them move in the house. If you can really trust your agent, they can also collect the rent for you, and then pay off the balance in your account. Finally, with an agent to help you out, you will not have to deal with the hassle of maintenance and repairs, and will also avoid having to attend to the tenant's complaints.

Ignoring insurance

Since selecting an insurance plan is not a legal necessity, and it is time-consuming, many people do not bother purchasing one. However, as we have learnt before, getting landlord's insurance is a crucial back-up plan. Some dangers of not investing in an insurance policy include:

- Loss of rent.
- Theft.
- Legal costs in case of hiring a lawyer.
- Property damage.

The hidden costs

Many people do not realise that managing property is more expensive than obtaining and repaying the mortgage! That is why it is necessary to emphasise again that you should count your costs before going ahead with an investment.

Summing Up

- There are numerous pitfalls landlords face in the buy to let market. In order to be successful you must be shrewd and have the foresight and effective planning needed to avoid these pitfalls.

- Usually you'd expect finance to be the biggest potential pitfall, however in some cases it can be the financer who is the bigger stumbling block. So always ensure you've done everything necessary to satisfy the lender so you obtain the finance.

- No matter how tempting a bargain on a below market value (BMV) property may be, it is not always wise to invest in these as a big saving can sometimes hide a big problem, such as structural issues, that may end up costing you more than you saved initially!

- Keep décor and furnishing simple so tenants can add their own personal touch, rather than making the property suit your taste – which may put others off.

- Always make accurate and realistic rental estimates based on your property and what it offers, avoid basing estimates on comparisons with similar properties as these may have different features that require a different amount of rent to be charged.

- Avoid purchasing multiple properties only because of discounts.

- Be thorough in your checks on potential tenants, review bank details and previous references to ensure you find tenants that will be both reliable and respectful in terms of payment and property.

- Avoid getting into problems with tax by ensuring you understand all the tax implications and regulations; hiring a qualified professional to sort your taxes for you will help you do this.

- Just as hiring an accountant will help you avoid issues with taxes, enlisting the services of an experienced letting agent can help you avoid many of the potential pitfalls landlords face.

Chapter Seven

Ten Things to Consider When Buying to Let

1 – Research

When you are new to any industry, you can't take the first step without conducting adequate market research. You have to make sure that you conduct both primary and secondary research. Reading facts, figures, and statements provided by others is necessary but not sufficient. Most importantly, you are ultimately responsible for the decisions you make, and you cannot blame anyone else. Therefore, research is one of the most crucial things to consider before you buy to let.

Of course, there will be times when you have to work with mere guesses, but research helps to minimise the chances of such occurrence. When you rely on an agent and follow him blindly, there may be a chance that you are being fooled. Some developers and promoters will lure you, but they are working on commission and they may not value ethics as maximum sales is their main aim.

You have to research the best property for letting. A good property to be researched is one with a high demand because profit is the main aim. When you are in the property business, you will frequently come across the mantra 'location, location and location'. This signifies the prime importance of location in the property business. However, what is location worth if it attracts no tenants? Therefore, demand is as important as location.

'You have to research the best property for letting. A good property to be researched is one with a high demand because profit is the main aim.'

The location can influence the demand, but tenants may also like to rent houses in places where traditionally landlords do not consider investing. Keep all options open. What sells is the right property. Another thing you must remember is that you are not the only one who is looking for favourable locations and properties. There are other property hunters out there as well. Keep the competition factor in mind as well.

Seeking tenants is another part of marketing for a buy to let investor. Never make estimates based on supply (cheap rates in a particular location), but only on demand. Keep your target market in your mind when you conduct this type of research so there is no confusion. You should not look for beach houses for students, or studio apartments for families! Of course, you wouldn't make this mistake, but this was just an illustration to make a point.

'Location is arguably the most significant factor when it comes to making profits from property investment.'

Research means to discover something, and this means that when you are out there searching the rental market, find out what is happening *right now* instead of what has happened or what will in the future. Once again, knowledge of past and future trends is good and you must gather it. But demand keeps fluctuating, and therefore it is better to buy a property to let if it currently has good demand.

Things that can help you in your research are:

- The Internet, where you can find many property websites with up-to-date information.
- Newspapers that have a separate property section.
- Separate weekly and monthly property publications.
- Property auctions and window displays.
- Local letting agents listings.
- Personal visits to different areas in the city.

2 – Location

Location is as important as anything else in the buy to let business. It is arguably the most significant factor when it comes to making profits from property investment. You have to carry out effective research to discover the areas where there is a high demand for rental housing. Do not be swayed by a low purchase price and buy the property, as the location may not look attractive to the tenants and you will be left with an empty property.

Another thing you should look for when considering a location is the amount of properties listed there for rent. You can do this easily at home by searching the Internet. But it would be better to make a physical effort and drive or walk by the location to see the amount of listings. If the number is great, then it could mean that the demand is high in the area and you should look for a buy to let property there.

On the other hand, a high amount of listings can also mean that the houses take quite a while to be let out, and there is a high level of saturation. A good way to determine the demand is to see for how long the listed houses have been on the market. Furthermore, if there are quality schools in a particular location, young families will be attracted. Find out such a location, and enquire about the rental housing performance in that area.

The presence or absence of local amenities also makes a lot of difference. If there is a location where shopping centres, parks, schools and hospitals are easily available, then there will be a high demand of tenants. People like to live in places where facilities like banks and post offices, as well as leisure outlets like pubs are in close proximity.

Crime rates also influence the choice of location. The best way to find out about the crime rate in a particular area is to ask the people who live there. The Internet is also a good place to research about crime rates in different areas in the city, and you can always visit the local police station. It is obvious that anyone who has the option will never choose to rent a house in an area that is known for its high crime rate, even if the rent is low.

Job opportunities

What else influences the choice of location? Chances of employment. This includes most people, especially graduates who would like to live in places from where they can easily reach their workplaces or places where job opportunities are widely available. In fact, many people shift from their old homes and look for new places that provide ease of commuting as well as chances of employment. A great way to capitalise on this factor is to find a location that will be near the city centre, but not the main city. That way, ease of transportation can be achieved while problems like congestion, traffic, noise and air pollution can be easily avoided.

3 – The property

Apart from the location, the property itself is a highly vital component to generate the maximum rental yield possible. Usually, from the landlord's point of view, the right kind of property is the one that is economically suitable. It should have a reasonable price and the rental income should be fairly good. You should spend some time probing around such properties on the Internet, newspapers, or even communicating with other owners and estate agents.

'Usually, from the landlord's point of view, the right kind of property is the one that is economically suitable. It should have a reasonable price and the rent income should be fairly good.'

But there is also the tenant's point of view that must be considered. This is because the tenant is the one who will be living inside the property, and if they are not getting what they want, then it will certainly affect your rental income. That is why you should never keep your personal preferences in the forefront while searching for the right kind of property. Try to walk in the tenant's shoes and look at things from their perspective.

This also means that any improvement that is done in the house should also reflect the needs of the tenants rather than the choices of the landlord. Although it is good to find the best deal on your available finance when you are purchasing the property, you should not always go for the cheapest. Also, view discounts and bargains with caution. You also have to decide whether you will buy newly built properties or older ones.

Instinct always tells you that you should go for the brand new ones, but that can prove to be expensive, and it is possible that the developer will charge you above the market rate. On the other hand, some people like old properties, like Victorian-style cottages. You may find more clients by spending less on old houses and you may also have a hard time finding people to rent your expensive, brand new apartment.

When it comes to used houses, you can come across ex-council properties as well that were once under municipal control. You can get a good deal here, but make sure that you thoroughly view the location before you purchase it. Maybe it is not big enough for families to live in. The choice of the property will largely depend on who you are targeting. Families will have different requirements, whereas foreign students will not mind staying in cheap rooms that may not be otherwise tenant attractive.

The general qualities of a suitable property

When you have selected a property for purchasing, you should enquire about its rental history. How much did the previous owners charge? Moreover, what was the tenant turnover rate? If tenants came and left at a notable pace, then suspect that there is something wrong with the property. However, it could also mean that the tenants were unable to pay their rents on time.

The size of the property is another thing that you should look for. Once again, keep the requirements of the tenants at the back of your mind while looking for a house. If you are targeting a family with little children, you will require a house with the suitable number of rooms to accommodate them comfortably, and if possible, there should be a garden as well.

Finally, you should also find out how old the property that you are going to purchase is. If the property is 20-25 years old, then you should not hesitate to purchase it. These properties usually do not have maintenance problems that even older buildings do. If an old building requires a lot of repair and renovation, then it is better to brush it aside. Remember, the onus is on you to fix all the issues, and charging a high rent to compensate this is not a practical option.

Furnishing

Another choice that you have to make will be about furnishing your property. It is considered that a fully furnished house will make the landlord secure, both legally and financially. However, that is not always the case. Nowadays, property owners only provide the basic supplies such as:

▒ Clean and furnished bathroom(s).

▒ Washing machine.

▒ Refrigerator.

- Carpets and curtains.
- Basic furniture.

Of course, as we move into the city centre, the definition of 'basic' furnishing would change altogether. On the other hand, tenants like students would do well even if all these facilities are provided properly as they rent the room/ house on a short-term basis. Hence, keeping a well-balanced property that is not under or over supplied is the best option for landlords.

So all the necessary 'preparations' you have to make for the tenants would simply include painting the walls and setting up clean and durable curtains and carpets. You also have to ensure that all the appliances are in proper working order. A word of advice is necessary here. When you are choosing the colours for the walls and the carpets, go with *neutral* ones. This will give the residents the freedom to personalise the house in their own way.

'Keeping a well-balanced property that is not under or over supplied is the best option for landlords.'

You may not find plain colours attractive, but remember what you learnt about personal choices. You may have a hard time coming to terms with it, but it is a fact that tenants like neutral furnishing. Since you are providing the furniture, you also have to supply the tenants with adequate cushions, mattresses and pillows that are made in compliance with safety regulations.

This also holds true for electrical wiring and gas pipes. It is the duty of the landlord to thoroughly check them and have the safety certificates issued by the relevant authorities.

4 – Finance

What is an investment without finance? Merely researching and planning will get you nowhere, unless you have the financial resources to purchase the property(ies). A buy to let mortgage is the source of finance that you use to purchase properties that are available for rent. It is mostly akin to the usual residential mortgage. The only difference is that this source of finance is availed for the aim of earning a profit.

That is why you should consider a buy to let mortgage as an investment rather than a liability. In theory, the whole process is quite simple, and is and is as follows:

- You apply for a loan.

- You obtain it.

- The house is purchased.

- The tenants move in and pay the rent.

- The payment over time will be sufficient to pay off the mortgage.

Anything apart from this simple process (like wealth generation through the sale of a house) is considered a bonus. Buy to let mortgages have increased significantly throughout the UK in recent years as the housing market has become a profit-making industry. Mortgage finance and buying to let are now considered great investment options by many. See chapter 1 for further details.

Of course, as in all borrowing, you need to have collateral against the mortgage amount. Usually it is the house that you live in (the principle residence), but it can be any other property as well. You can find loans for repayment, or interest-only mortgages as well. Check your financial position thoroughly before applying for the loan.

Finance for holiday lettings

Selecting the adequate finance is also an important factor when you invest in holiday homes for letting. You may have done your research well and found the right spot for the holiday letting, but have you decided the source of finance? It is true that financial matters are not easy to comprehend, and most people do not know how to even begin arranging the money.

The local market scenario is different, but when you are investing in a foreign property, you should definitely go for an agent or a broker. They will know the local market far better than you, and they will help you get the best mortgage deals. Of course, there are black sheep in all circles, but that does not mean that good brokers cannot be found.

A financial agent will not control your money, but will guide you in the best deal possible. Local mortgages are quite complex, so you can well imagine the mental hassle that you will experience when you research about holiday mortgages. If you personally think that financial dealing is not your cup of tea, then you should definitely consult an expert to avoid any serious difficulty.

You should also remember that in order to apply for a buy to let holiday mortgage, your property needs to be compatible with certain requirements, otherwise you will not get the loan and the property will not get the status of a holiday home. The requirements are as follows:

- The house should be available for public renting for at least 140 days a year.

- Out of the available days, it should be occupied for 70.

- All rentals will be short term.

- The tenant cannot live there for more than 31 days.

- The property cannot be let out to the owner's relatives and friends on cheaper rates.

Some lenders will provide the mortgage based on your personal income most likely from a job. Others will simply look at the estimated rental income, and they will base their decisions on these calculations. This is one area where a broker can really help you.

Finally, you should know that although a broker or an agent is helping you out, the decision ultimately lies in your own hands. Take out the time to gather all the necessary information there is pertaining to buy to let investments. Another thing that will definitely contribute to your success as a landlord is creativity. Learn to think for yourself, and always be on the search for new horizons.

This is the actual success story of some of the wealthiest people in the world. Remember, if you cannot take serious decisions about matters like financial arrangements, you may as well give up the idea of investment altogether.

5 – Tenants

Location, property and finance. Everything ready? But all these things together cannot make you a profit unless you find the tenants. This is one of the most crucial things to consider when you engage in buy to let. Make sure that you promote at the proper places to find potential clients and compel them to live in your property. You should check the tenants thoroughly and gather as much information as possible about them.

'Another thing that will definitely contribute to your success as a landlord is creativity. Learn to think for yourself, and always be on the search for new horizons.'

Good relations between the landlord and the tenant are also necessary, because the tenants will be living in your property for quite a while. If you are employing a letting agent, be sure that their fee falls in your budget. You should also seek legal help when drawing up any agreements.

Finding the right tenants

Decide what kind of tenants you want to find. If you are targeting students, you can easily find the demand for rental homes by consulting their accommodation authority. Universities usually cannot house all their students, and they do appreciate these rental schemes. They are, however, adamant that the rental homes should have all the basic necessities as well as security measures.

On the other hand, professionals would like to live in close proximity to their workplace. For example, nurses and doctors would love to find a place that is close to their hospitals, as it would help them avoid extra commuting time to compensate for their informal working hours.

Advertising for tenants

Sure, you can post on the Internet or in newspaper advertising sections, but most people do not realise that word of mouth is also an effective way of finding tenants. Try to bring up your property in your conversations, and you will be surprised to see how many potential tenants you can find. Moreover, if the location is a small town, you can even post advertisements on notice boards at the local post office.

Remember, this is *direct* marketing. You have to communicate everything personally for the most part in order to win customers. You can always chat with estate agents or property managers to understand the local market and what the tenants are really looking for. Better still, get in contact the people in your target area and try to find out what they really want in a house.

'Make sure that you promote at the proper places to find potential clients and compel them to live in your property. You should check the tenants thoroughly and gather as much information as possible about them.'

The property itself can serve as a great promotion tool. The more features a house has, the greater the chance of finding tenants at your desired rates. For example, houses that have a garage or lawn (or even both) will be loved by both professionals and young families and you will be in a better position to negotiate a higher rent.

Finally, when you are posting online or advertising in newspapers, make them persuasive rather than simply informative. Do not just list the features of the house, but try to emphasise as much as you can all the benefits that people will receive if they choose to live in that house. Appeal to their needs and emotions, and you will be able to attract the perfect tenants.

6 – Tax

Tax is yet another crucial aspect of buying to let you should seriously consider before joining the industry. New landlords will especially find buy to let tax information both tough and confusing. Another thing that keeps most people thinking is whether they should operate their buy to let business personally or as a limited company. Both choices have tax implications.

If you want to avoid paying income tax on your rental income, you can run your buy to let business as limited company. In this case, you should not withdraw the profits out of the company, but re-invest them in the business. This way, the value of the company will rise, yet the level of tax will not. Generally speaking, small property companies only have to pay 19%. This is, however, the corporate tax but as you know, dividends have to be paid out in a limited company, and the recipients will be subject to income tax. This can be as high as 25%. Also, if the buildings are sold and the company faces closure, you will be charged the capital gains tax on the sale proceeds, which can move your tax bracket up to 40%.

On the other hand, when you run your buy to let business under your personal name, you have to pay income tax on the rents you receive. While making estimates of the profits you are likely to make, remember that any interest you pay on your buy to let mortgage will be offset against your profits for deducting income tax.

This is one major reason why most of the buy to let landlords opt for mortgages on an interest-only basis. You can further reduce your tax bill by counterbalancing the costs you incurred during the repairs and maintenance of your property before calculating the tax. Therefore, it is highly advisable that you retain the invoices or the bills you pay during home improvement.

As you know, you have to pay capital gains tax when you sell your property. However, there is also a way to mitigate the tax bill. Most landlords gain a relief on this profit tax by declaring (and proving) that they themselves were living in their property. It is not completely illegal, as the law stipulates that if you live in a property yourself, you can get up to three years relief on the tax when you plan to put it up for sale.

Finally, you should know that not everyone is a specialist when it comes to taxation laws, and there is nothing wrong in that. Fortunately, there are some people who study these laws minutely, and consulting these specialists (lawyers, agents, accountants) will definitely help you avail every opportunity for tax relief. See chapter 4 for more details.

7 – Management

Your responsibility as a property owner is not over even when the tenants move in. The job of the landlord virtually never finishes. Apart from taking care of the property, you also have to deal with the people who live in it. So this is not only a game of money, you have to invest your time and energy as well. Remember that always.

Hired help

However, you can always carry out all the management responsibilities through a professional letting agency. In this way, you will literally outsource the tasks of finding the tenants and looking after them. The cost of the agency is usually fixed on a percentage of the monthly rental earnings. When you go for this option, you will benefit from the services of experienced individuals who are proficient in dealing with property and tenancy issues.

'Your responsibility as a property owner is not over even when the tenants move in. The job of the landlord virtually never finishes.'

You will also be relieved of the stress of money management. All the payments and bank deposits will be carried out by the agency. Most importantly, agencies tend to know the rental market really well, and therefore they can strike the best deal for you. Although the cost can be high when you base it on your monthly earnings, you will discover that hiring an agent is economically efficient in the long run.

Another way of managing your property is though collaboration with a third party. This means the agent will look for the tenants, move them in and draw up their agreements, but you will take over from here. In this scenario, the day-to-day management, as well as rent collection and legal procedures will fall on your shoulders. This option will save you a lot of money, and it will enhance your abilities as a good landlord.

However, new landlords may not have the necessary knowledge and experience that is required for property management, and they might make some mistakes if they do not take the help of experts.

'As a landlord, you should only spend money on things that will benefit you monetarily in the long run.'

Go it alone

The third and final way of managing your property is doing everything on your own. Primary responsibilities include:

- Marketing the house.
- Finding the tenants.
- Managing the tenants.
- Dealing with property repairs and maintenance.

This option is the best for those landlords who are looking for the maximum returns from their buy to let investment. Since no third party is involved, all the earnings will directly fall in their pocket. However, once again, this is not a viable option for a new landlord, who literally knows nothing about the job of being a landlord.

Which is best?

In our opinion, the second form of management, where you collaborate with an agent, is the best one to choose. It helps you benefit from professional help, but also provides opportunities for self-growth. Remember the thing about balancing your investment and earnings. As a landlord, you should only spend money on things that will benefit you monetarily in the long run. A letting agency should also be selected on this principle, i.e. whether it takes more money or helps you earn more. You will automatically move towards increased self-reliance as you gain more experience and as you expand your business as a property investor.

8 – Insurance

One thing that landlords, especially the young and inexperienced ones, overlook is insurance. However, this is not a healthy attitude, and there are many significant reasons that can persuade anyone to draw up an insurance plan. Property investments particularly should be covered by insurance as fluctuations in the market as well no earnings can leave a proprietor in a financial mess.

Most property owners who are planning to invest in buy to let, and many who already have done so, do not consider the fact that even after the house is given out on rent they are responsible to get a building insurance plan. Your tenants will usually be responsible to take care of their own belongings and the things they own (such as interior decoration) via insurance, but this depends on the tenancy contract. However, even if this is the case, the tenants are not supposed to insure the entire building. That burden lies on your shoulders.

One of the most widely known insurance among property owners offers coverage in cases where the tenants fail to pay their rent on time. Ask yourself, do you have the financial capacity to go on for three to four months without receiving any rental income? Of course, this is the worst that can happen, but it *does* happen. How will you handle the mortgage payments when you are not gaining anything economically from the house you bought?

'One of the most widely known insurance among property owners offers coverage in cases where the tenants fail to pay their rent on time.'

Moreover, if your tenants are not paying their rent on a regular basis, you would naturally have to force them to leave. As easy as it sounds, tenant eviction can prove to be a thorn in the flesh that you simply cannot get rid of, even after trying really hard. But even if you do succeed to empty your property of the bad tenants, imagine how long it can take to replace them with new ones. Again, it is also possible that you find fresh occupants immediately, but in the worst case scenario, you would have to go for a considerable amount of time without any real income.

Think well before skipping the idea of insurance. Of course, the decision will depend on your personal financial situation which may allow you to go on without generating any rental money. But ponder upon these matters before planning an insurance policy.

'Most landlords do not consider all the possible costs while calculating the profits or the rental yields.'

If you do realise the need for insurance, then get the landlord insurance policy which is a coverage plan for property owners. It protects them from financial set-backs that do happen when the property is occupied by tenants. There a few basic features of a buy to let property insurance that you should keep in mind.

Firstly, you will get coverage on the contents inside the rental property that will be used by the tenants. Items like electric appliances and sofas will be protected from serious damage and/or stealing. Secondly, there is a liability cover than helps the landlord to pay any claims made in cases of an injury to a tenant or even his/her death. Finally, there is a building insurance cover that financially helps the property owner in times of repairs or rebuilding. See chapter 5 for more details on insurance.

9 – Costs

Apart from your tax and utility bills, there are several other costs that you would have to pay as a buy to let landlord. Before the actual trading begins, you make estimates of the likely income that you will earn and the expenses you will bear to bring home that money. However, most landlords do not consider all the possible costs while calculating the profits or the rental yields.

A simple way of making these calculations is that you calculate the total rental income for the year and deduct all the possible operating expenses. This amount will then be divided by the original value of the house. For example, if the value of a house is supposedly £15,000 and the total rent minus expenses is £6,000 (£7,500-£1,500), then yield will be (6,000/15,000) 0.4%.

However simple this method appears, you can have low income and high costs in reality. How is that possible? Notice that there are two basic errors in this calculation. Firstly, the value of the house is only based on its market or purchase price. However, you will have to pay some additional expenses to acquire the house, which include:

▨ Mortgage deposit.

▨ Legal costs.

▨ Costs of survey and inspection.

▨ Furnishing.

Since you have to make these payments to get the property, they should logically be included in the value of the house when you calculate the yield. Another error is that many significant costs that usually have to be paid in the first few months of the tenancy have completely been ignored. Some of these expenses include:

▨ No income because tenants cannot be found.

▨ No income because tenants have failed to pay the rent.

▨ Commissions paid to the letting agency (usually 10% plus value added tax).

▨ Insurance premiums.

▨ Ground rent.

▨ Sundry costs, such as phone bills and fuel.

Even when you include these figures, the final answer will still be a guess of what you are likely to earn. However, when you do make these considerations, you can have a more accurate picture of your financial position in the first year of tenancy.

'As of February 1997, any tenancy agreement will be based on the Assured Shorthold Tenancy Agreement.'

10 – Legal issues

This is the final thing that you have to consider before buying to let. Even as a landlord, you have to play by the rules because any lawsuit filed against you can possibly ruin your property investment career for life.

The buy to let industry has grown over time in the UK, but the laws are still not as detailed as you would find in other property sectors. This does not mean that comprehending these laws is easy, and the market is flourishing with new regulations being passed. At this time there are around 50 Acts of Parliament dedicated to buying to let. Therefore, you should get familiar with these laws before embarking on the journey of property investment.

If you are afraid to put in the tremendous effort of going through law books to learn about these regulations, you can always get some help. You can join landlord groups and associations or hire the services of a lawyer. One of the legal requirements is that you draw up a tenancy agreement with the tenants before they start to live in your property. As of February 1997, any tenancy agreement will be based on the Assured Shorthold Tenancy Agreement.

This will provide you the legal ability of evicting the tenants easily once their agreed term ends. The tenancy agreement will specify things like the payments of deposit, the dates of renewal, the responsibilities of both parties, etc. As of April 2007, any deposit taken by the tenant will be regulated by the tenancy deposit scheme. If the owner does not join this scheme and yet requires a deposit from the tenants, he/she can face legal action which can result in fines and even loss of property.

Furthermore, the landlord is also obligated by the law to conduct safety checks inside the rental property on a regular basis and obtain all safety certificates from the respective authorities. Finally, the landlord should not harass or exhibit discrimination while dealing with the tenants.

Remember that even if you are doing your duty well, an undesirable tenant can threaten you legally for no apparent reason. Legal proceedings can put a serious burden on your pocket. That is why you are advised to obtain an insurance policy that also covers legal costs.

Summing Up

- This chapter focused on ten important factors that need to be considered critically for the best chance of success in the buy to let market.

- As discussed in previous chapters, issues such as research, location and selecting the right tenant(s) have to be considered carefully. Gathering useful research and choosing the correct location and tenant(s) are vital components in a successful rental business.

- The complexities of buy to let laws and regulations, tax implications and insurance plans should be understood and adhered to accordingly. A good knowledge of these can help landlords save money through tax relief, and effective insurance policies guard against loss of income, amongst other things. Adhering to the laws of buying to let means you should never find yourself in any awkward positions regarding lawsuits and difficult evictions.

- It is important not to overlook the additional costs involved in a buy to let venture. For example, when calculating the value of the property don't forget financial factors such as legal costs and the mortgage deposit that played a part in the actual cost of it.

- Probably the best way to manage your investment is to work with an agent who will deal with finding the tenants and drawing up the necessary agreements, leaving you to take over from there. Meaning your responsibilities will include the day-to-day management, collection of rent, legal procedures, etc. This method works well in the long run as it saves money and broadens your skills and experience as a landlord.

- Finally, it is important to remember, as we keep emphasising, help is available with virtually every aspect of the buy to let process. Expert advice on matters like tax can often prove to be invaluable.

Chapter Eight

Looking Forward: A Resurgent Market

The change of events

If there is anything that can be blamed for destroying the hype and popularity of buying to let, it is the recession. During this period, interest rates rose to great heights and the number of people who were willing to continue property investment decreased. But now, there is a turning of the tide. The situation is changing as it has become possible to find properties at reasonable rates.

Buy to let investors are returning back to the market in increasing numbers. The market for rented houses is gaining its charm again, with both investors and lenders willing to play the buy to let game. Rental income is also reaching a new high, which helps to make property investment an attractive business once again. That, however, does not mean that all investments are likely to succeed.

'Buy to let investors are returning back to the market in increasing numbers.'

Figuring out the finance

To ensure the maximum gains on your venture and to avoid yet another loss, you have to understand the essential details of buy to let mortgages. When you are looking for loan finance you will come across a plethora of different offers and types of mortgages available in the market. That is why when you plan to make an investment in a buy to let property, thoroughly review all the options that are placed before you to find the best mortgage.

You know very well that when you opt for a buy to let mortgage, you will have to pay a higher interest as compared to a residential mortgage. Likewise, the terms and conditions pertaining to buy to let mortgages also differ from your standard housing loan. The lender will have a completely different criterion by which he would judge the buyer.

What are some of the things that a mortgage lender looks for?

Firstly, a finance provider will examine your credit history. Nobody wants to lend out a mortgage to a person who is a defaulter on paper. Secondly, the lender will also look at the estimated rental value of the property. This is because the rent is the main source of money from which the mortgage will be repaid, and if it is not enough (usually less than 125% of the mortgage amount), then he is likely to reject the application.

Another point to remember is that if the borrower has another mortgage on their own home, then the amount of the buy to let mortgage that will be issued (if it is passed) will be significantly lower than under normal circumstances. The lender will also be interested to know whether you have the financial capacity to make the monthly payments or not.

It is a known fact that many tenants often fail to make their payments on time. How will you, the lender will ask, make the mortgage payments under these conditions? You must have a good answer to convince the lender and obtain the loan. With all the background clearly laid, understand that although the mortgage finance is the most crucial component of a buy to let investment, it is also the most critical one as well.

If you have any confusion related to the current mortgage deals and interest rates, you can always contact a specialist mortgage broker who is proficient in all the details related to buy to let finance. You will also be able to find the best mortgage deal, and the investment opportunity that can provide short or long-term gains.

Rental demand

Even statistics are showing the signs of resurgence in the buy to let market. Different surveys exhibit the same trend, including one conducted by the CML which states that buy to let lending increased by 32% between the first quarter of 2011 and 2012. The market has still not touched its 2007-2008 peak, but there is hope that it will.

After the global recession (or 'credit crunch'), buying to let was greatly tapered. But optimistic analysts say that this factor gives the market a greater potential for coming back on its feet. Moreover, lending in this segment has also increased since the past year. Lenders believe that although buy to let investments run the same risks as housing mortgages, the returns on property investment outweigh the risks.

By charging high rates, lenders can make fairly good profits at low loan to value (LTV). The risks, at least in theory, in buying to let are slightly greater than normal house loans. When a person fails to pay the mortgage on a personal residence due to adverse economic conditions, he/she can jump here and there to look for a solution. One the other hand, a buy to let landlord will face a dilemma, as he/she would have two properties to save – the principle residence, as well the rental property. The landlord would instinctively try to arrange money to protect their own house, and therefore may lose the investment completely.

But even with these grave implications, the prospective returns are enough to compel a person to go ahead with investment. The owner would earn from the rents that tenants pay, as well as benefit from capital gains when they sell the property, and the lender would benefit from monthly payments if a tenant defaults.

Another significant factor that has caused the resurgence of buying to let is the high rental demand. Demands are quite high nowadays, with yields going up to 5-6%, depending on the city or the area you have purchased your property in. The high rental yields will help to lower the chances of non-payment by the tenants. Back in the peak period, the high house prices helped the rental market to grow. However, at this time, it is the limited supply of finance that has kept existing landlords from leaving.

'Buy to let lending increased by 32% between the first quarter of 2011 and 2012. The market has still not touched its 2007-2008 peak, but there is hope that it will.'

This is the nature of the buy to let market. When housing prices are falling, landlords will go for the cheap property to expand their portfolio. Rental yields may fall at times of high accommodation rates, but the owners can always sell the property to earn great returns. The rebirth of the industry has already caused many lenders to lower the LTV, and it is possible to find a lender who has softer lending rules.

The debt factor

With all the good news giving a heads-up to landlords, new investors might still find it difficult to find a loan. Much depends on the interest rates set by the Bank of England which can both encourage and hinder property purchase. Buy to let investments have risen at impressive rates in the past few years, but debts caused by these investments are also not hidden.

'Another significant factor that has caused the resurgence of buying to let is the high rental demand.'

Many landlords have come under significant debt. However, new investments can generate good returns that can reverse this situation. Increased inflow of cash can help many landlords come out of their debts if they conduct proper financial planning. If you are already under this problem you should strive to make larger repayments on your loan from the high rents you are receiving at present. This can also improve the LTV of your building, which will be really beneficial in times of falling prices. Many properties have suffered in this manner.

That is why debt management is necessary. Be on guard against rising interest rates, and, if possible, re-negotiate the terms of your mortgage to adapt to the current economic situation. It is not impossible to find mortgages that can adapt to higher interest rates. Another way to improve your cash flow situation is to increase your rental rates. That way you will some reserve cash as well for any unforeseen problem. High rental rates are a great way to come across void months when no rent is paid.

Summing Up

- The ultimate conclusion of this book is that even though the road is not 100% safe, you can still travel a long way by equipping yourself well. And that was the aim of this essential guide, to equip you in all facets of the property investment business so that you can earn the greatest returns.

- The recession of recent years is probably the biggest cause of the decrease in popularity of buy to let investments.

- However, at the time of writing, statistics have shown a significant increase in buy to let lending, making the market a more attractive place for investors old and new.

- High rental demand has played a big part in the resurgence of the buy to let market. Also, falling house prices have meant a growth in rental property as landlords snap up cheap property to add to their portfolios.

Glossary

Assured Shorthold Tenancy

Is the set limit on a tenant's staying term for houses in England and Wales. It was introduced by the Housing Act of 1988, and further changes were made under the Housing Act of 1996. This law provides limited security of tenure and the ease of legal eviction.

Below market value (BMV) properties

Properties that can be bought at what appears to be a great bargain, however hidden problems can sometimes see any initial savings quickly used up in repairs.

Buy to let

The term that refers to the purchase of a property with the intention of renting it out.

Capital gains tax

Capital gains tax is levied on the sale of a buy to let property, but only if the property is not the owner's principle residence.

Cap on rent

'Cap' is short for the capitalisation rate. It is the ratio between the net profit produced by an asset and its purchase price or market value. In our case, the asset is the buy to let property.

Cash flow

In business terms, cash flow describes the movement of money in and out of a business. Cash inflow is the cash you receive (such as rent), and cash outflow describes the factors that take money out of the business (agency fees, etc.).

Gross and net income

Gross income is the amount of money you earn from which the taxes and other expenses have not been deducted. After these deductions, the remaining income is called the net income. For example, the monthly rent you receive directly from the tenant is the gross income. After paying all the bills (like mortgage interest), the amount that will be left will be your net income.

Income tax

This is charged on a person's net income, i.e. rent for a landlord.

Liquidity

Liquidity is the ability of an asset or a security to be purchased or sold in the market while retaining its value. It is a term used in increased trading activity, where assets that can be bought or sold rapidly are considered to have liquidity. To put it in another way, liquidity is the ability of an asset to rapidly convert into cash.

Outsource

When you hire an external group or an individual to look after any aspect of your business it is known as outsourcing. In buying to let, the letting agent can be a good example of outsourcing.

Rental yield

Similar to the capitalisation rate, the rental yield simply describes the return on an investment.

Retail price index

The retail price index is an index used to measure the level of inflation (rising prices) in the UK. It is published every month by the Office for National Statistics, and it uses particular commodities (known as a basket of goods) to measure rates of inflation.

Help List

Association of Residential Letting Agents (ARLA)

Arbon House, 6 Tournament Court, Edgehill Drive, Warwick, Warwickshire,
CV34 6LG
Tel: 0845 250 6001
www.arla.co.uk/buy-to-let/buy-to-let-information/
ARLA is a self-regulating professional body catering to the needs of residential
lettings and letting agents. You will find detailed and updated information on
buying to let from their website.

Association of Residential Managing Agents (ARMA)

178 Battersea Park Road, London SW11 4ND
Tel: 020 7978 2607
www.arma.org.uk/
Based in England and Wales, ARMA is a trade association for companies that
deal in private residential leasehold block of flats.

Atlantis Group

22/24 Market Place, Reading, Berkshire RG1 7RG
Tel: 0118 956 6464
headoffice@atlantisgroup.co.uk
www.atlantisgroup.co.uk/
Atlantis Group deals in property sector and businesses with the aim of coming
up with new entrepreneur solutions.

The Building Societies Association

6th Floor, York House, 23 Kingsway, London WC2B 6UJ
Tel: 020 7520 5900 (Consumer information)
www.bsa.org.uk/
The Building Societies Association is body that represents mutual lenders and
deposit takers all over UK.

Carter Jonas

127 Mount Street, Mayfair, London, W1K 3NT
Tel: 020 7493 0676
Email: mayfair@carterjonas.co.uk
www.carterjonas.co.uk/
Carter Jonas is firm based in England and Wales that specialises in property consultancy, surveying and estate agent services.

CKD Glabraith

59 George Street, Edinburgh, EH2 2JG
Tel: 0131 240 6960
Email: Edinburgh@ckdglabraith.co.uk
www.ckdgalbraith.co.uk/residential
CKD Galbraith is a Scottish property consultancy firm that also specialises in sales and letting of private properties.

Connells

Cumbria House, 16-20 Hockliffe Street, Leighton Buzzard, Bedfordshire, LU7 1GN
Tel: 01525 218500
complianceresidential@connells.co.uk
www.connells.co.uk/
The Connells Group is a firm that operates in asset management along with sales and property mortgage services.

Council of Mortgage Lenders

Bush House, North West Wing, Aldwych, London WC2B 4PJ
Tel: 0845 373 6771
www.cml.org.uk/cml/home
CML deals with home financing, especially mortgage lending in the UK.
Contact them to receive the latest updates on what's happening in the buy to let market.

Countrywide

Countrywide House, Clerkson Street, Mansfield, Nottinghamshire, NG18 1BQ
Tel: 01623 665100
www.countrywide.co.uk/
Countrywide is UK's largest and most successful property service group. They offer property letting solutions as well.

The Coventry Building Society

Economic House, High Street, Coventry, CV1 5QN
Tel: 0845 766 5522
www.coventrybuildingsociety.co.uk
Coventry TLC is a building society based in Coventry.

Edinburgh Solicitors Property Centre

ESPC, 85 George Street, Edinburgh, EH2 3ES
Tel: 0131 624 8000
Email: help@espc.com
www.espc.com/
ESPC is a property marketing company based in Edinburgh.

National Association of Estate Agents (NAEA)

Arbon House, 6 Tournament Court, Edgehill Drive, Warwick, Warwickshire, CV34 6LG
Tel: 0845 250 6001
www.naea.co.uk/about-us
NAEA provides quality assistance to property owners in the UK. They provide estate agent services to new property dealers as well.

Northern Rock

Northern Rock plc, Mortgages, Northern Rock House, Gosforth, Newcastle Upon Tyne, NE3 4PL
Tel: 0845 602 8301 (for existing customers)
Tel: 0800 0285 277
www.northernrock.co.uk/
Northern Rock is a British Bank which is run by Virgin Money. By visiting their website, you can find information on their various mortgage products.

RH & RW Clutton

East Grinstead, 92 High Street, East Grinstead, West Sussex, RH19 3DF
Tel: 01342 410122
www.rhrwclutton.com
RH & RW Clutton is an established property surveying firm, operating since
1743.

Whelan

Whelan Commercial Limited, Arthur House, 41 Arthur Street, Belfast, BT1 4GB
Tel: +44 (0)28 9044 7144
Email: email@whelan.co.uk
www.whelan.co.uk
Whelan Commercial is a property consultancy firm in Belfast, UK regulated by
the Royal Institution of Chartered Surveyors.

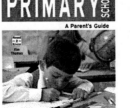

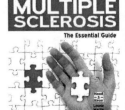